DEPRESSION

AND ITS TREATMENT

The American Psychiatric Press, Inc., an independent corporation affiliated with the American Psychiatric Association, publishes psychiatric literature for professionals. This book is one of many titles planned for publication which expands the scope of the Press into publications of interest to the general public. The first three to be released include:

How You Can Help: A Guide for Families of Psychiatric Hospital Patients
   By Herbert S. Korpell, M.D. (casebound) #48-016-5 $15.95;
   (paperback) #48-026-2 $9.95

Depression and Its Treatment: Help for the Nation's #1 Mental Problem
   By John H. Greist, M.D. and James W. Jefferson, M.D.
   (paperback) #48-025-4 $7.95

The American Psychiatric Association's Psychiatric Glossary (paperback)
   #48-027-0 $7.95

1400 K Street, N.W.
Washington, D.C. 20005

DEPRESSION

AND ITS TREATMENT
Help for the Nation's #1 Mental Problem

By John H. Greist, M.D. and James W. Jefferson, M.D.

American Psychiatric Press, Inc.

1400 K STREET, N.W.
WASHINGTON, D.C. 20005

Note: The authors have worked to ensure that all information in this book concerning drug dosages, schedules and routes of administration is accurate at the time of publication and consistent with standards set by the United States Food and Drug Administration and the general medical community. As medical research and practice advance, however, therapeutic standards may change. For this reason, and because human and mechanical errors sometimes occur, we recommend that readers follow the advice of a physician directly involved in their care or the care of a member of their family.

Library of Congress Cataloging in Publication data
Main entry under title:
Greist, John H.
    Depression and its treatment.

    Includes index.
    1. Depression, Mental. I. Jefferson, James W.
II. Title.
RC537.G733 1984   616.83′27   83-25666
ISBN 0-88048-025-4

Printed in the U.S.A.

To the memory of
Mary Ann Jerse, M.D.
1954-1983

Contents

About the Authors

Drs. Greist and Jefferson are trained as internists as well as psychiatrists. They are now professors of psychiatry at the University of Wisconsin Medical School in Madison.

Dr. Greist is director of the Phobia and Other Anxiety Disorders Clinic and co-director of the Lithium Information Center with Dr. Jefferson. He is co-author with Thomas Greist of *Antidepressant Treatment: The Essentials*, published in 1979 (Williams and Wilkins).

Dr. Jefferson is director of the Center for Affective Disorders. He and Dr. Greist have co-authored two successful professional books on lithium, *Primer of Lithium Therapy* (Williams and Wilkins, 1977) and *Lithium Encyclopedia for Clinical Practice* with Deborah Ackerman (American Psychiatric Press, Inc., 1983). They also edited *Treatment of Mental Disorders* with Robert L. Spitzer (Oxford University Press, 1972).

Dr. Greist and Dr. Jefferson both are regular runners and have five children (two of whom are sick at any given time), two wives (both healthy), seven living grandparents, two dogs, three cars, countless bicycles, and the usual array of problems that affect humankind.

Acknowledgments

This book is the result of contributions from many doctors and patients. We can acknowledge the doctors by name and take pleasure in doing so:

From the Department of Psychiatry at the University of Wisconsin:

Richard Anderson, Nancy Barklage, Ronald Diamond, Burr Eichelman, Robert Factor, Carl Getto, John Marshall, William McKinney, Paulette Selmi, Steven Sorrell, Pierre Tariot and Steven Weiler.

From elsewhere:

John Howard Greist and Thomas Greist of Indianapolis, Indiana, and Joseph Tally of Grover, North Carolina.

Our patients carefully read and criticized drafts of the book. They suggested many of the subjects addressed and the questions asked and answered. We appreciate their important perspective as much as we admire their courage and resilience in facing depression.

Georgia Greist and Bill Marten sharpened their editors' pencils to clarify our cryptic exposition and expunge our medical metaphors and jargon. It is obvious they did not work on the previous sentence.

Jean Clatworthy prepared the numerous drafts of this book. Her attention to detail, efficiency and good humor in the face of deadlines are constant qualities that enhance our effectiveness.

American Psychiatric Press has in two short years become a major publishing house for psychiatric titles. We admire the professionalism of the staff and appreciate the simultaneous care and speed with which they work. Special thanks are due Richard E. Farkas, whose compulsivity at proofreading matches ours. We take pleasure in sharing responsibility with him for errors in spelling and syntax while retaining responsibility for decisions about content and emphasis.

INTRODUCTION

This book is for:

People being treated for depression
People considering treatment for depression
People wondering whether they are depressed
Families and friends
Those who treat depressed patients
And anyone else interested in depression

It is a guide to understanding:

Depression
What depression is not
How depression is treated
Treatment side effects and how they are managed

We wrote it because we know:

Doctors* sometimes forget to ask patients about important information

Doctors sometimes forget to advise patients about important facts

Patients sometimes forget important information

Patients sometimes misunderstand important instructions

We hope it will:

Maximize the recognition and proper treatment of depression

Minimize treatment difficulties

Promote the best results for patients

John H. Greist
James W. Jefferson
Madison, WI
February, 1984

* We often use the word "doctor" to indicate psychiatrists and other medical doctors (M.D.'s), as well as psychologists who have doctor of philosophy degrees (Ph.D.'s). M.D.'s can prescribe antidepressant medications as well as provide all other treatments for depression including psychotherapy while psychologists use only psychotherapy.

WHAT IS DEPRESSION?

Depression means different things to different people. Depression can be a *symptom* (as when a person says, "I feel depressed"), a *sign* (when someone observes, "his expression looks depressed"), or a diagnosable *disorder*. When we diagnose *depression*, we mean a disorder of sufficient length with specific symptoms and signs which substantially interferes with a person's functioning or which causes great personal distress — or both.

It is important to separate depressive disorders from everyday "blues" or sadness which are not depression. Normal grief accompanying the death of a loved one is not depression either. People with the blues or normal grief may experience short-lived symptoms of depression but usually continue to function almost normally and soon recover without treatment. From here on, when we use the term *depression* we mean the *disorders of depression* which need treatment.

Depression requiring treatment affects:

mood or "spirits"
thinking (cognition)
bodily functions
behaviors

Mood in depression is almost always experienced as sad, blue, "down in the dumps," worried or depressed. If mood does not appear depressed, a person may lose interest or pleasure in most activities. Sometimes mood lifts temporarily when a depressed person receives good news. Sometimes it does not. Doctors sometimes use the word *"affect"* instead of *mood*, and they mean essentially the same thing when referring to depression.

Depressed *thinking* often takes the form of *negative thoughts* about one's self, the present and the future. Depressed people also frequently complain of poor concentration, poor memory, and difficulty making decisions. *Anxiety*, a sense that something unspecified but dreadful may happen, is often present. Exaggerated fear about specific situations may also occur. As depression becomes more severe, patients often think they are helpless and worthless and their situation is hopeless. They often think of suicide. In the most severe depressions, delusions (false beliefs that are rigidly held even in the face of strong evidence to the contrary) may appear, sometimes involving themes of crimes the person has never committed or serious physical illness which is not present or poverty when that is not the case. Occasionally, hallucinations (sensations for which there is no external cause) may occur. These are usually experienced as hallucinations that are heard (usually voices, but sometimes music, clicks or other noises) or seen (images of people or flashes of light) and occasionally by hallucinatory experiences of taste, touch or smell. These most severe depressions are sometimes referred to as "psychotic" depressions, and hallucinations and delusions and poor judgment indicate that the person has "lost contact with reality."

Bodily or *"vegetative" functions* may be affected in depression. Patients commonly experience appetite disturbance (either decreased appetite with resulting weight loss or, less frequently, increased appetite with weight gain); sleep disturbance (usually difficulty falling asleep and/or frequent awakening and/or early morning awakening with inability to fall asleep again, but sometimes increased sleep); fatigue (see page 15); decreased energy; lessening of interest in usual activities, including sex; and gastrointestinal symptoms such as dry mouth, nausea, constipation or, less commonly, diarrhea. Pains sometimes mysteriously appear, may migrate from one site to another and disappear when depression lifts (see page 41).

Behavior changes associated with changes in mood, thinking and bodily function may vary from those which are minor and largely unrecognized to profound problems with obvious tearfulness, sad expression, stooped posture, and slowed down or agitated movements, pacing, restlessness, wringing of hands, etc. Some people are able to work normally but feel horribly depressed; others are unable to perform daily activities like dressing, eating, washing or working because of depression. At times, depressed patients may put on a smile in an attempt to cover their depression—the so-called "smiling depression." The most extreme example of depressed behavior is suicide.

Physicians and laymen from antiquity to the present have recognized depression and described it clearly.

Hippocrates told of a woman "of a melancholic turn of mind, from some accidental cause of sorrow [who] while still going about became affected with loss of sleep, aversion to food and had thirst and nausea."

Robert Burton's *Anatomy of Melancholy* appeared in 1621 and remains a lucid description of depression, showing as well how depression has been a part of mankind's experience through the years: "If there be a hell upon earth, it is to be found in a melancholy man's heart."

"Melancholy," an ancient term, continues to be used to describe very severe depression with loss of pleasure in enjoyable activities, failure to feel better when something good happens, depression regularly worse in the morning, early morning awakening, slowed or agitated physical activity, loss of appetite or weight loss and excessive or inappropriate guilt.

Hamlet's depression is clear in Act I, Scene 2:

> "Oh, that this too too solid flesh would melt,
> Thaw, and resolve itself into a dew!
> Or that the Everlasting had not fixed
> His canon 'gainst self-slaughter! Oh, God! God!
> How weary, stale, flat, and unprofitable
> Seem to me all the uses of this world!
> Fie on 't, O fie! 'Tis an unweeded garden,
> That grows to seed,
> Things rank and gross in nature
> Possess it merely."

Alexander Haig, a physician writing in 1900, caught the essence of severe depression: "In this condition self-reliance is absolutely gone, extreme modesty is common or even habitual, a feather weight will crush one to the dust, and even the greatest good fortune will fail to cheer."

Unknown or famous, patients describe depression with similar poignance (this patient quote and the one from Joshua Logan are reproduced with permission of William Morrow and Company, publisher of *Moodswing*):

> "Prior to this I had been overly happy, elated because of having given birth to lovely twins two months earlier. At first I tried to keep my mind occupied by keeping busy around the house, cleaning, and taking care of the babies. However, I soon had no enthusiasm for anything. I seemed to get no pleasure out of living. I had no feeling toward the babies or my other two children. I tried to do extra things for the children because I felt extremely guilty about my lack of feeling. I would do everything in the house quickly and then would find myself with nothing to do. I had no interest in any outside activity or any project which would be of great interest to me in a normal frame of mind. I

couldn't concentrate. My mind seemed to be obsessed with black thoughts. My husband took me out frequently to take my mind off things, but even that was an effort for me.

"As time passed, these feelings of despair and uselessness increased. I lost ten pounds and had no appetite. I would try to sleep away time but found myself unable to. I had terrible dreams and would wake up often throughout the night with a feeling of panic in the pit of my stomach. This feeling of anxiety was always present, and for no good reason it continued to get worse. I found myself not wanting to go back home when I went out to try to shop, yet I couldn't be alone. No matter what I did, I couldn't concentrate except on questions such as, 'What is the matter with me? Am I going insane? What have I done to deserve this? What sort of punishment is this?' I felt that my appearance had severely changed. I felt old and unattractive. I had no sexual desire and became more and more guilty about my lack of sexual interest in my husband. I wondered if I was going through the menopause. Could the change of life make me feel such tension and anxiety?

"Eventually I found myself going to sleep earlier at night and wanting to sleep as much as possible. This was the only way my mind would stop thinking the same anxious thoughts over and over again. Shortly after this I began to feel physically ill, my appetite got worse, and my smoking increased. My stomach began to trouble me, and I developed severe daily headaches. One day on awakening I found myself unable to get out of bed. Because I felt physically sick and unable to care for my family I began to think that I had a virus and asked my husband to call the family doctor. He gave me a thorough physical exam with blood tests and urinalysis, and found nothing wrong, but I persuaded him to treat me for a virus anyway. He didn't mention that this might be a masked or hidden depression, with anxiety and physical pain my only complaints.

"Several days later, after taking medication, I felt no better, and I awoke the next morning and felt that I didn't want to live. Nothing in life seemed important or worthwhile, and I thought of ways to commit suicide. These thoughts racked my entire body with fear. I knew then that I was not physically sick and that I had to reach out for another kind of help. I told this to my husband and saw my physician again. Upon hearing what I had to say, this time he prescribed an antidepressant and a tranquilizer. He didn't seem to know too much about what depression was or what kind of medication was needed. He recommended that I see a psychiatrist, which, of course, I couldn't possibly do. After taking the medications for one day I felt even worse. If I had to see a psychiatrist, it meant that I was probably going insane, and this thought made me even more frightened. It was more than I could stand. The fear of being mentally ill was so horrible that I decided to take my entire bottle of sleeping pills rather than face the shame of being a mental patient."

Joshua Logan has helped many people recognize that depression (in his case manic-depression) is compatible both with great suffering as well as great productivity after recovery:

"My first impression was that something had sneaked up on me. I had no idea I was depressed, that is, mentally. I knew I felt bad, I knew I felt low. I knew I had no faith in the work I was doing or the people I was working with, but I didn't imagine I was sick. It was a great burden to get up in the morning and I couldn't wait to go to bed at night, even though I started not sleeping well. But I had no idea I had a treatable depression. I had no idea it was anything like a medical illness. I thought I was well but feeling low because of a hidden personal discouragement of some sort—something I couldn't quite put my finger on. If anyone had told me that I could walk into a hospital and be treated by doctors and nurses and various drugs and be cured I would have walked in gladly and said, 'Take me,' but I didn't know such cures existed. I just forced myself to live through a dreary, hopeless existence that lasted for months on end before it switched out of the dark-blue mood and into a brighter color. But even then I didn't know I had been ill.

"It seemed to me that all friends of the average human being in depression only knew one cure-all, and that was a slap on the back and 'buck up.' It's just about the most futile thing that could happen to you when you're depressed. My friends never even hinted to me that I was really ill. They simply thought that I was low and was being particularly stubborn and difficult about things. If anyone had taken charge and had insisted that I go to a mental hospital, I probably would have gone straight off. Instead they simply said, 'Please don't act that way. Please don't look at your life so pessimistically; it's not so bad as you think. You'll always get back to it. Just buck up.'"

Abraham Lincoln also knew depression well:

"I am now the most miserable man living. If what I feel were equally distributed to the whole human family, there would not be one cheerful face on earth. Whether I shall ever be better, I cannot tell; I awfully forebode I shall not. To remain as I am is impossible. I must die or be better, it appears to me."

WHAT CAUSES DEPRESSION?

Depression is almost always caused by a combination of factors. Inheritance or genetic predisposition, developmental factors such as early loss of a parent, environmental stressors such as difficulties in a marriage or at work and physiological stressors such as illness or complications of treatment of illness all combine to produce a final common pathway to the disorder of depression. Each individual has a pattern of genetic, developmental, environmental, social and physiological factors which combine to permit or protect against depression at any point in time. Understanding and modifying the contributions of these factors is the goal of clinicians who treat depression.

It is now clear that *genetic factors* are important in many cases of depression. If one identical twin has depression, there is a 70 percent chance that the other twin will also develop depression at some time. Children, parents, and brothers and sisters (including non-identical twins) of a depressed person have only a 15 percent chance of developing depression. More distant relatives (grandparents, uncles, aunts) have about a 7 percent risk. The risk for people without close relatives who have had depression is about 2-3 percent. Decreasing risk of depression with decreasing genetic similarity supports the idea of inheritance of depression.

Another line of genetic research points to the same conclusion. When children whose parents have a history of depression are adopted at birth into families without any history of depression, they are three times more likely to develop depression than natural children of the adopting family.

A few people who experience *early losses* of important persons may develop some predisposition to later development of depression. Thus, children who lose parents at an early age and do not find a suitable replacement may be prone to develop depression in later life.

Humans are social animals and if *relationships* are difficult and loneliness extreme, depression sometimes develops. Conflicts with family members, employers, co-workers, employees, friends and even acquaintances can all take their toll. Death is clearly a major social stressor although at times, as when someone is painfully and terminally ill, it can be a relief. Grief does not usually develop into depression.

Religious preoccupations and worries about the meaning of life may contribute to or aggravate depression. Religion may also be a source of support and comfort and provide meaning during depression.

Many *environmental stressors* such as financial problems, new jobs, legal problems, retirement, or other changes *possibly* contribute to the development of depression.

Medical illnesses such as influenza, mononucleosis, hepatitis and too much or too little thyroid hormone as well as several *medications* (including various blood pressure lowering medications, birth control pills and steroids such as cortisone) can cause or contribute to depression.

It is important to recognize that these are risk factors and are not guaranteed to cause depression. Some people who become depressed have experienced many of these risk factors. Others have experienced none that can be identified even after careful evaluation. Many people who have one or more risk factors for depression *never get depressed*. Much remains to be learned about the causes of depression.

Depression can also *cause* impaired relationships, job problems, financial stress — many of the things that some people feel bring on depression. But even when the causes are unclear, treatment can help most depressed people. The disruptive effects of depression can be severe and it is important that depressed persons not be blamed for a medical disorder they cannot control.

WHAT ARE THE CHANCES
OF DEVELOPING DEPRESSION?

Several studies done in different American communities have found that about 5 percent of the population can be diagnosed as having major depression at any one point in time (see pages 25 to 28 for a description of *major* depression). At least 10 percent of the population will experience a major depression during their lifetime (some studies find rates up to 25%). Women are one and a half times as likely to become depressed as men. Studies in many countries and cultures and across all social classes show a similar frequency of depression. People with a history of serious depression have on the average about five episodes during their lifetime although the number of episodes varies greatly and some people will have only a single episode while others may have many more. Early treatment can decrease the length and severity of depression for most people.

At least 10 percent of people with depression will also have manic episodes, and they are said to have "manic-depressive" or "bipolar" disorder. During mania, mood changes from its normal level to an elevated, expansive, elated or even euphoric state which patients often describe as being "on top of the world." During a manic episode a person may sleep very little, talk continually and very rapidly, take little time to eat, show marked irritability and impatience and feel as though his or her thoughts are racing. Often the manic state progresses to a point where judgment is impaired and contact with reality is lost. It may be difficult to understand what a person is saying. Sometimes poorly thought-out decisions are acted on impulsively, with serious financial, social or occupational consequences for self, family and others. Hospitalization may be necessary. See page 55 for a discussion of lithium and its role in the treatment of manic-depressive disorder.

THE DEPRESSIVE SPECTRUM

Although *depression* means a depressive disorder of specific length with specific symptoms and signs, some people find it helpful to think of the different kinds of depression as occurring on a spectrum from mild blues or sadness at one extreme to severe, life-threatening depression at the other. Although people sometimes say they are depressed when they are actually feeling blue, sad or even normal grief, these *symptoms* are *not the disorder of depression* as we define it and these people usually require no treatment. As people move to the right across the depressive spectrum, they enter the area where the *disorder of depression* and the need for treatment begin. The further to the right one moves along the depressive spectrum, the more severely depressed the person is.

Many doctors use the depressive spectrum as a way of explaining the difference between just feeling bad and the disorder of depression. This perspective is shown in Figure 1. This approach organizes useful information about duration of depression, effect on functioning, symptoms, possible causative factors and treatment choices.

SUMMARY

Depression is widespread and common. Serious depression affects 5 percent of the population at any point in time, and at least 10 percent of the population will experience a major depression at some point in their lifetime. About 10 percent of people with major depression will end their lives by suicide.

Although depression spares no segment of the world's population, treatment can restore many sufferers to lives of sensitivity, creativity and accomplishment.

Many factors are thought to contribute to the develop-

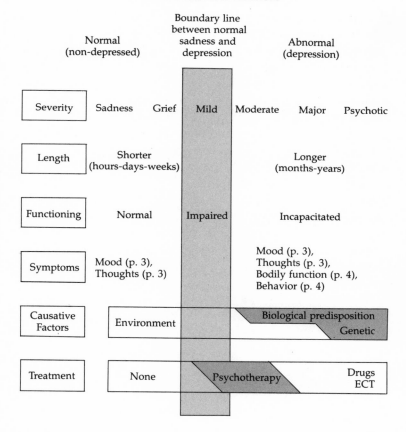

Figure 1
THE DEPRESSIVE SPECTRUM*

*Adapted with permission from Diagnosis of Affective Disorders (p. 222) by Frederick R. Goodwin in the chapter *Psychopharmacology in the Practice of Medicine*, Murray E. Jarvik (ed.), Appleton-Century-Crofts, New York, 1977.

Figure 1 represents a way to symbolize depression. It inevitably oversimplifies the complex phenomenon of depression. Thus, there are individuals who have a comparatively mild depression (see the severity category above) that lasts for years (length category) and probably have a genetic predisposition to develop depression (causative factors). Other patients will have very severe but short depressions. Depression is simply not fully understood at this time.

ment of depression. Depression probably appears when several factors combine in particular ways that are not yet well understood. The occurrence of many different combinations partly explains the many different forms of depression.

QUESTIONS ABOUT DEPRESSION

Is depression a chemical imbalance? In the end, the answer is, *probably yes*. All of our feelings and thoughts, both pleasant and distressing, are the result of many electrochemical reactions that occur throughout our brains and bodies. Our present understanding of these reactions and the multitudinous interactions among them is incomplete. It's as though it is the year 1400 and we are setting out to discover what continents and peoples exist and how they are related to one another.

We have learned, however, from past experience and early studies of psychopharmacology, that most depressions can be treated with chemicals called antidepressant medications. Our understanding of the mechanisms of action of these drugs is incomplete, but together with electroconvulsive therapy (ECT), they are the most effective treatments available for depression. Although how they work is not fully known, it seems fair to conclude that antidepressant medications and ECT work by correcting "chemical imbalances."

Is depression caused by something bad happening in a person's life? Sometimes it is possible to identify a specific event which appears to have produced depression. Even when this appears to be the case, the depression frequently seems too severe a reaction for the event which appeared to bring it on. Often, depression seems to come on for no reason. This happens to people whose lives are going well and to people who are having trouble in some area of their lives. It may be that people who develop depression because of genetic vulnerability are more susceptible to bad things that happen in their lives.

Is depression inherited? It now appears clear that some people have an inherited predisposition to develop some forms of depression. On page 7 this issue is covered in some detail.

How common is depression? Depression is very common —the most common of all mental disorders. At any one time, about 5 percent of the population is suffering from a major depression. Throughout our lifetimes, at least 10 percent of us will experience a major depression. Depression is ten times more common than schizophrenia (characterized by disorders of thinking such as hallucinations and delusions, and by alterations in speech and behavior, some of which may be bizarre) and three to five times more common than the major anxiety disorders (phobia, obsessive-compulsive disorder and panic attacks).

Community surveys suggest that only half of the people suffering from major depression are treated. Failure to receive treatment can result in substantial losses of time from work and pleasure in life and family, and to death by suicide.

Do children get depressed? Children certainly do get depressed, although they may not show depression in the same way adults do. For example, sad mood in children may not be described in words but can be seen in persistent sad expressions. Instead of the weight loss seen in adults, children may fail to gain weight as expected. Rather than loss of interest in usual activities or decrease in sexual drive noticed by adults, children may simply show signs of apathy or not caring. Other signs of childhood depression may include acting out, or other behavioral problems and eating disorders, that lead to great weight loss or gain.

Families often notice changes in children as they become depressed. School work may fall off and previously energetic and boisterous children may become fatigued and quiet. When depression is suspected, the child should be evaluated by a doctor experienced in working with children and depression. Depression in children can be as severe as in adults (adolescent suicide has increased sharply). Children require and respond to the same treatments used with adults.

What role does fatigue play in depression? All problems seem worse when we are tired or fatigued and a good night's sleep usually puts things into a more realistic perspective. Lady Macbeth properly praised "sleep that knits up the raveled sleeve of care." With depression, sleep is often difficult and seldom relieves fatigue even if the person sleeps for many hours. The fatigue of depression is unrelieved by rest and sleep and depressed people must struggle with the continuous burden of fatigue. Antidepressant treatment, not rest or sleep, is the cure for fatigue caused by depression. It is possible, though not certain, that fatigue which builds up as a result of too many pressures or from ignoring our body's needs for "good food, fresh air, rest and exercise—the quadrangle of health" may contribute to the development of depression.

Can hypoglycemia cause depression? Hypoglycemia or

low blood sugar can cause emotional symptoms such as anxiety, sweating, shakiness, weakness, lightheadedness and fatigue. These symptoms, however, are more often due to other causes. Symptoms of depression are only *very rarely* due to hypoglycemia. The unfortunate tendency to overdiagnose hypoglycemia often results in inappropriate treatment and hides the correct diagnosis. The *properly conducted* measurement of blood sugar (often a glucose tolerance test) is a necessary part of a hypoglycemia evaluation.

Can allergies cause depression? A lot of controversy surrounds this issue. Although recent studies have shown that food hypersensitivity can cause psychological symptoms in some people, there have been no conclusive studies which prove that allergy causes depression. A movement known as clinical ecology holds that illnesses (including depression) are often caused by hypersensitivity or "allergic" reactions to a wide variety of environmental substances. The mainstream of medicine, however, regards such claims as extravagant and unsubstantiated. Well-designed research studies are needed to resolve this controversy. One such study scientifically tested a group of patients who believed that food allergy caused many of their medical and psychological symptoms. Only 17 percent actually had hypersensitivity to food and none of them had psychological symptoms.

Can hormone imbalance cause depression? Yes, but depressive symptoms usually occur as part of a group of other findings that suggest a particular hormonal disorder. Occasionally this is not the case and depression may be the only finding. At other times, depression and a hormonal disorder may occur at the same time but be unrelated.

Hormonal or endocrine disorders that may cause depressive symptoms include thyroid gland underactivity (hypothyroidism) and very rarely overactivity (apathetic hyperthyroidism); underactivity (Addison's disease) or overactivity (Cushing's syndrome) of the adrenal gland; underactivity or overactivity of the parathyroid gland (disordered calcium metabolism); and the premenstrual syndrome. Hormonal drugs such as oral contraceptives (birth control pills) and steroids (cortisone, prednisone, etc.) may occasionally cause depressive symptoms.

If depressive symptoms are due to a hormonal abnormality, they will be relieved when the abnormality is corrected. A comprehensive evaluation of depression should include attention to the endocrine system.

What can I do to fight depression? It depends. If depression is mild, if other aspects of your life are in good order (relationships, occupation, health, etc.) and if you are able to participate regularly in interpersonal (page 38) or cognitive psychotherapy (page 39) or to exercise (page 63) on a regular basis, you might recover from a mild depression. Sometimes depression stops without treatment after enough time has passed, usually several months or even a few years. More often, even with mild to moderate depression and almost always when depression is severe, *you will need help* in the form of medication to overcome depression.

How effective are treatments for depression? Very effective! The first antidepressant medicine you and your doctor try has about a 70 percent chance of helping. Cognitive and interpersonal psychotherapies may also be effective for less severe depressions. If the first treatment fails, other effective treatments are available. No one has real reason to fear that his or her depression is untreatable.

Are antidepressant medicines the same as tranquilizers, pep pills, "uppers," sleeping pills, pain pills, sex

pills or nerve pills? NO! Antidepressant medicines stand in a class by themselves. Antidepressant medications counteract anxiety, pain, decreased energy, loss of sex drive and sleep disturbance, but do so by treating the underlying depression which causes all of these symptoms. In this way, the body's normal functioning is restored.

AM I DEPRESSED?

Everyone has unpleasant experiences which can lead to feelings of sadness or the blues. Most of these feelings are short-lived and go away when the unpleasant experiences stop or when better ways of dealing with problems are found. The boundary line between normal blues or sadness and depression which requires treatment is not sharply defined. Some patients seek treatment for sadness which disappears spontaneously in a few days. Some physicians withhold treatment until they are absolutely certain that depression is present. These different boundary lines for deciding when to seek and to offer treatment are understandable considering our current knowledge about depression.

Most professionals agree that depression should be treated if it causes sustained interference in general social functioning or in intimate relationships or educational or occupational functioning. Many agree that treatment should be considered when personal suffering from depression reaches a distressing level for the individual even though he or she is able to handle most life situations. In the end, decisions regarding the need to treat depression are best made on individual grounds by patient and doctor. Severe depression may seriously impair the patient's judgment and decision-making ability. When disagreements arise, involvement of the family, the passage of time or a second opinion from another doctor may relieve the uncertainty.

If we accept that disagreements remain about defining and diagnosing depression, what help is available for identifying depression? A number of self-report, paper-and-pencil questionnaires have been developed to help with general *screening* for depression. Of the several available questionnaires, the Beck Depression Inventory (BDI) has gained greatest acceptance in the United States. It was copyrighted by Dr. Aaron T. Beck in 1972 and is reproduced with his permission.

BECK DEPRESSION INVENTORY

This questionnaire contains groups of statements. Please read each group of statements carefully. Then pick out the *one* statement in each group which best describes the way you have been feeling the PAST WEEK, INCLUDING TODAY. Circle the number beside the statement you picked. If several statements in the group seem to apply equally, circle the highest number. *Be sure to read all the statements in each group before making your choice.*

1. 0 I do not feel sad.
   1 I feel sad.
   2 I am sad all the time and I can't snap out of it.
   3 I am so sad or unhappy that I can't stand it.

2. 0 I am not particularly discouraged about the future.
   1 I feel discouraged about the future.
   2 I feel I have nothing to look forward to.
   3 I feel that the future is hopeless and that things cannot improve.

3. 0 I do not feel like a failure.
   1 I feel I have failed more than the average person.
   2 As I look back on my life, all I can see is a lot of failures.
   3 I feel I am a complete failure as a person.

4. 0 I get as much satisfaction out of things as I used to.
   1 I don't enjoy things the way I used to.
   2 I don't get real satisfaction out of anything anymore.
   3 I am dissatisfied or bored with everything.

5. 0 I don't feel particularly guilty.
   1 I feel guilty a good part of the time.
   2 I feel quite guilty most of the time.
   3 I feel guilty all the time.

6. 0 I don't feel I am being punished.
   1 I feel I may be punished.
   2 I expect to be punished.
   3 I feel I am being punished.

7. 0 I don't feel disappointed in myself.
   1 I am disappointed in myself.
   2 I am disgusted with myself.
   3 I hate myself.

8. 0 I don't feel I am any worse than anybody else.
   1 I am critical of myself for my weaknesses or mistakes.
   2 I blame myself all the time for my faults.
   3 I blame myself for everything bad that happens.

9. 0 I don't have any thoughts of killing myself.
   1 I have thoughts of killing myself, but I would not carry them out.
   2 I would like to kill myself.
   3 I would kill myself if I had the chance.

10. 0 I don't cry any more than usual.
   1 I cry more now than I used to.
   2 I cry all the time now.
   3 I used to be able to cry, but now I can't cry even though I want to.

11. 0 I am no more irritated now than I ever am.
   1 I get annoyed or irritated more easily than I used to.
   2 I feel irritated all the time now.
   3 I don't get irritated at all by the things that used to irritate me.

12. 0 I have not lost interest in other people.
   1 I am less interested in other people than I used to be.
   2 I have lost most of my interest in other people.
   3 I have lost all of my interest in other people.

13. 0 I make decisions as well as I ever could.
   1 I put off making decisions more than I used to.
   2 I have greater difficulty in making decisions than before.
   3 I can't make decisions at all anymore.

14. 0 I don't feel I look any worse than I used to.
   1 I am worried that I am looking old or unattractive.
   2 I feel that there are permanent changes in my appearance that make me look unattractive.
   3 I believe that I look ugly.

15. 0 I can work about as well as before.
    1 It takes an extra effort to get started at doing something.
    2 I have to push myself very hard to do anything.
    3 I can't do any work at all.

16. 0 I can sleep as well as usual.
    1 I don't sleep as well as I used to.
    2 I wake up 2-3 hours earlier than usual and find it hard to get back to sleep.
    3 I wake up several hours earlier than I used to and cannot get back to sleep.

17. 0 I don't get more tired than usual.
    1 I get tired more easily than I used to.
    2 I get tired from doing almost anything.
    3 I am too tired to do anything.

18. 0 My appetite is no worse than usual.
    1 My appetite is not as good as it used to be.
    2 My appetite is much worse now.
    3 I have no appetite at all anymore.

19. 0 I haven't lost much weight, if any, lately.
    1 I have lost more than 5 pounds.
    2 I have lost more than 10 pounds.
    3 I have lost more than 15 pounds.

    I am purposely trying to lose weight by eating less
    _____ yes _____ no

20. 0 I am no more worried about my health than usual.
    1 I am worried about physical problems such as aches and pains; or upset stomach; or constipation.
    2 I am very worried about physical problems and it's hard to think about anything else.
    3 I am so worried about my physical problems that I cannot think about anything else.

21. 0 I have not noticed any recent change in my interest
         in sex.
     1 I am less interested in sex than I used to be.
     2 I am much less interested in sex now.
     3 I have lost interest in sex completely.

The BDI is scored by adding the numbers of the separate items selected. Do not score weight lost on purpose (item 19). A score of 0-9 would be considered in the normal range, 10-15 would suggest mild depression, 16-23 would be consistent with moderate depression, and a score of 24 or more suggests marked depression.

We feel anyone who scores between 10 and 23 should repeat the BDI in two weeks. If the score is still between 10 and 23, and particularly if it has risen, a doctor should be consulted for an evaluation. If the score is greater than 23, a prompt evaluation is certainly indicated. If the score is less than 10 but other indications of depression exist, evaluation is also wise.

It is important not to depend too heavily on outside measures of depression. Although they can add some objectivity to the assessment of depression and permit comparisons with a large population of individuals with depression, the *subjective experience of depression* is highly variable. Some people with normal scores on a depression questionnaire are severely depressed and respond dramatically to treatment.

DIAGNOSIS AND DSM III

Questionnaires such as the BDI are *not diagnostic of depression* but are helpful as screening devices. Diagnoses of depression are now made on the basis of criteria contained in the *Diagnostic and Statistical Manual of Mental Disorders, Third Edition* (DSM-III) of the American Psychiatric Association (1980). DSM-III is designed for *use by clinicians* and was not written for patients. Although we list various depressive disorders as defined by DSM-III in Appendix A of this book, we feel it is helpful for patients to see an example of the criteria of one kind of depression, namely, *major depression* which is the common diagnosis for depression requiring treatment. The criteria are as follows:

A. Dysphoric mood or loss of interest or pleasure in all or almost all usual activities and pastimes. The dysphoric mood is characterized by symptoms such as the following: depressed, sad, blue, hopeless, low, down in the dumps, irritable.
The mood disturbance must be prominent and relatively persistent, but not necessarily the most dominant symptom, and does not include momentary shifts from one dysphoric mood to another dysphoric mood, e.g., anxiety to depression to anger, such as are seen in states of acute psychotic turmoil. (For children under six, dysphoric mood may have to be inferred from a persistently sad facial expression.)

B. At least four of the following symptoms have each been present nearly every day for a period of at least two weeks (in children under six, at least three of the first four).
1. poor appetite or significant weight loss (when not dieting) or increased appetite or significant weight gain (in children under six, consider failure to make expected weight gains)
2. insomnia or hypersomnia
3. psychomotor agitation (pacing, restlessness, hand wringing, etc.) or retardation (slowed movements) (but not merely subjective feelings of restlessness or being slowed down) (in children under six, hypoactivity)

4. loss of interest or pleasure in usual activities, or decrease in sexual drive not limited to a period when delusional or hallucinating (in children under six, signs of apathy)
5. loss of energy; fatigue
6. feelings of worthlessness, self-reproach, or excessive or inappropriate guilt (either may be delusional)
7. complaints or evidence of diminished ability to think or concentrate, such as slowed thinking, or indecisiveness not associated with marked loosening of associations or incoherence
8. recurrent thoughts of death, suicidal ideation, wishes to be dead, or suicide attempt

C. Neither of the following dominates the clinical picture when an affective syndrome (i.e., criteria A and B above) is not present, that is, before it developed or after it has remitted:
1. preoccupation with a mood-incongruent delusion (see definition below) or hallucination
2. bizarre behavior

D. Not superimposed on either Schizophrenia, Schizophreniform Disorder, or a Paranoid Disorder.

E. Not due to any Organic Mental Disorder or Uncomplicated Bereavement.

With Psychotic Features. This category should be used when there apparently is gross impairment in reality testing, as when there are delusions or hallucinations, or depressive stupor (the individual is mute and unresponsive). When possible, specify whether the psychotic features are mood-congruent or mood-incongruent.

Mood-Congruent Psychotic Features. Delusions or hallucinations whose content is entirely consistent with the themes of either personal inadequacy, guilt, disease, death, nihilism, or deserved punishment; depressive stupor (the individual is mute and unresponsive).

Mood-Incongruent Psychotic Features. Delusions or hallucinations whose content does not involve themes of either personal inadequacy, guilt, disease, death, nihilism, or deserved punishment. Included here are such symptoms as persecutory delusions, thought insertion, thought broadcasting, and delusions of control, whose content has no apparent relationship to any of the themes noted above.

With Melancholia. Loss of pleasure in all or almost all activities, lack of reactivity to usually pleasurable stimuli (doesn't feel much better, even temporarily, when something good happens), and at least three of the following:

a. distinct quality of depressed mood, i.e., the depressed mood is perceived as distinctly different from the kind of feeling experienced following the death of a loved one
b. the depression is regularly worse in the morning
c. early morning awakening (at least two hours before usual time of awakening)
d. marked psychomotor retardation or agitation
e. significant anorexia or weight loss
f. excessive or inappropriate guilt

Other depressive disorders defined in DSM III are: Bipolar Disorder (manic-depression), Cyclothymic Disorder, Dysthymic Disorder, Schizoaffective Disorder, Adjustment Disorder with Depressed Mood, Uncomplicated Bereavement, Organic Affective Syndrome, Dementia with Depression, Substance-induced Affective Disorder, Atypical Depression and Atypical Bipolar Disorder. Each disorder has specific criteria for diagnosis and the process of diagnosis when done properly is quite complicated.

Diagnosis clearly requires careful consideration of many factors including the individual's past history, family history, response to treatment, present symptoms (what patients complain of) and signs (what doctors observe). The increasing complexity of psychiatric diagnosis is also providing increasing diagnostic accuracy. An open mind, strong powers of observation, continuing study of diagnostic advances, patience and experience combine to make an excellent diagnostician. If the diagnosis is not clear or if the response to treatment is less than satisfactory, both patient and doctor may benefit from a consultation or second opinion.

LABORATORY TESTS

Several new laboratory tests to identify depression are being evaluated. These tests attempt to identify markers of abnormalities in biological function that suggest a likelihood of depression. Blood, urine and sometimes spinal fluid are used in these tests. Measurement of brain waves by electroencephalogram (EEG) is also being studied.

All of these tests remain under development, but one (the dexamethasone suppression test—DST or DEX test), has reached a stage of development where some psychiatrists are using it with some of their patients. However, in about half of people with major depression, the DST is normal and these individuals usually respond as well to standard antidepressant medications as do those who have abnormal DST's.

Until the meanings of these tests are clarified, many conscientious physicians will continue to treat depressed patients successfully without using these tests.

SUMMARY

A diagnosis of depression rests on a careful history of present symptoms and past episodes, family history, observations of the patient by the physician (including physical examination), reports of family members and laboratory studies. *All of these factors must be weighed* in the process of coming to a decision about diagnosis and the need for treatment. At times, the diagnosis may be unclear and a further period of observation may be needed. At other times when the diagnosis is unclear, patient and doctor may decide to begin treatment because distress is of such magnitude that waiting is unjustified.

With the development of questionnaires like the Beck Depression Inventory, diagnostic systems like DSM III and great strides in the fields of epidemiology (study of the frequency and distribution of disorders), basic science and laboratory test research, both diagnosis and treatment are becoming more refined and successful.

WHAT ABOUT SUICIDE?

Suicide accounts for at least 25,000 deaths each year in the United States. This figure may represent a substantial under-reporting because of the social stigma attached to death by suicide or because of the possible loss of insurance benefits. Some experts estimate that as many as 75,000 people may commit suicide each year. Suicide is the major cause of premature death in psychiatric patients, and about three-quarters of those who commit suicide do so while depressed. About 12 out of 100,000 people in the United States commit suicide each year. Risk of suicide is greater in men than in women although women make more suicide attempts. Suicide risk increases with age, but suicide is the second cause of death (after automobile accidents) for young people. Although the suicide rate among young people is lower than in some other age groups, the number of suicides among 15- to 24-year-olds has doubled in the past 10 years and tripled in the past 20.

Prediction of suicide risk remains a difficult problem.

Even individuals with all of the most powerful predictors of suicide risk have only a 5 percent probability of committing suicide in the next year. Nevertheless, this risk is 500 times greater than the average risk in the population at large. Since any person with a substantial risk of suicide is likely to benefit from psychiatric treatment, recognition of major risk factors for suicide is an important part of the management of depression.

The factors listed below have the greatest *statistical* accuracy in predicting suicide risk. Statistical averages are difficult to apply to individuals because at times unusual factors are involved in an individual's decision to attempt suicide.

1. **Age.** Risk increases steadily with age for males and increases with age for females until about 70 when it reaches a plateau. Those over 65 make up 11% of our population but account for 25% of all suicides.

2. **Sex.** Males are three to four times more likely to die of a suicide attempt than females but females make three to four times as many attempts as males.

3. **Depression.** About three quarters of the people who kill themselves are depressed at the time they do so. Feelings of helplessness, or hopelessness or worthlessness or guilt about some real or imagined fault often lead to thoughts of suicide. About 10% of people with major depression end their lives by suicide.

4. **Previous suicide attempt.** Sixty percent of people who kill themselves have made a previous suicide attempt.

5. **Alcohol or other drug abuse.** Alcohol is the most widely available and most abused drug in our society. Alcohol and other drug abuse sometimes reflects attempts at self treatment of depression with drugs. Suicide may be precipitated by discouragement that

comes with a life complicated by drugs as well as confusion and loss of control associated with intoxication.

6. **Recent loss** of important persons, positions or possessions. This includes death or separation because of divorce, loss of a job whether through discharge or retirement and loss of prized possessions.

7. **Social isolation.** People living alone and without support of friends.

8. **Beginnings of recovery** from depression with renewed energy and determination in a person with previous thoughts of suicide.

9. **Clear plans** for committing suicide with a method that is likely to be lethal and access to the instruments of suicide.

SUMMARY

Depressed persons and those around them must be aware of the risk of suicide. The old saw about "people who talk about suicide never do it" is simply not true. Thoughts of suicide are common during depression and people with these distressing thoughts will often share them with those they trust. When a patient shares thoughts of self-injury or suicide, an assessment of suicide risk should be made by a professional. Most of the time, patients with suicidal thoughts can remain outpatients. Sometimes hospitalization is appropriate to reduce the risk of suicide.

HOW IS DEPRESSION TREATED?

Just as there are different factors which may cause depression, there are different treatments for depression. Sometimes these treatments are aimed directly at the presumed causes of depression. More often they are given because they have been shown to be generally helpful or because the doctor is most familiar with their use.

Psychotherapy is always appropriate in depression requiring treatment. Every patient should have the benefit of support and empathic understanding during the course of a depressive episode. **Supportive psychotherapy** also helps the doctor learn the effects of other treatments from the patient. Support and explanation should also be provided, with the patient's permission, to family members, friends and others important in the patient's life. These individuals constitute a network of support more available than anything the doctor can provide. When other treatments are ineffective, support by caring others can sustain a person until depression resolves on its own with the passage of time.

Other psychotherapies have more ambitious goals of effectively alleviating symptoms of depression, uncovering psychological causes of depression and helping the patient to insights and changes in personality characteristics and behaviors that may prevent recurrence of depression. See pages 37 to 40 for further information on psychotherapy for depression.

Medications are the cornerstone of treatment for major depressions. The effectiveness of antidepressant medications has been conclusively proven, but issues of selecting the best medication and minimizing side effects remain important. Pages 41 to 58 cover medications in more detail.

Electroconvulsive or "shock" therapy (ECT) has been maligned in recent years. ECT remains the single most effective treatment for severe depression, is most effective in lessening or eliminating suicidal risk and is sometimes helpful when other treatments have failed. ECT is described more fully on pages 59 to 61.

Other treatments such as exercise, sleep deprivation and psychosurgery are controversial and the subject of ongoing research. Each of these novel treatments appears to be useful for some patients. Please see pages 63 to 65 for more information.

All of the treatments mentioned above have a role to play in the treatment of depression. Selecting the best treatment for each patient requires knowledge, experience, skill and sometimes luck. When one treatment is ineffective, it is likely that another will be successful. Optimism that a successful treatment will be found, persistence in pursuit of a successful treatment and flexibility in matching patient with treatment are hallmarks of good treatment of depression. Each of these classes of treatment will be discussed in more detail in the following sections.

PSYCHOTHERAPY

Psychotherapy is sometimes referred to as "talk" therapy. Patients and their doctors talk about the experiences patients have had and are having, important relationships and future goals, as well as the feelings, thoughts and behaviors they produce. Psychotherapies are usually helpful for less severe depressions which form the largest part of the depressive spectrum. Psychotherapies are less effective for more severe depressions, but may be helpful in improving relationships or thinking patterns that may have led to depression. General support of depressed patients is always of benefit and may sustain them through their suffering even if other treatments are ineffective.

Although psychotherapies are frequently provided to depressed patients, there is less evidence supporting their effectiveness than is available in support of the effectiveness of antidepressant medications and electroconvulsive therapy. There are more than 100 specific named psychotherapies. However, most psychotherapies are variations on one of the following five approaches.

SUPPORTIVE PSYCHOTHERAPY

All patients need and deserve support while they are depressed. Supportive psychotherapy helps by shoring up defenses, utilizing strengths, empathizing with distress, explaining the course of depression, monitoring changes and reassuring the patient that improvement will, in time, occur. All doctors provide support to their patients. Family doctors often know the patient best and can therefore provide the most support.

DYNAMIC PSYCHOTHERAPY

Dynamic therapies seek to understand unresolved unconscious conflicts which may lead to depression. Depression is often described as anger turned inward, and it is felt that helping the individual uncover, understand and deal more appropriately with angry feelings may lead to recovery from depression. Interpretation of dreams, free association and exploration of the past are important techniques of psychoanalytic psychotherapy. Other psychodynamic psychotherapists may use the same techniques but focus more on present relationships and role functioning. Patients are helped to understand the possible role of these factors in their depression and to find new ways of dealing with people and feelings.

INTERPERSONAL PSYCHOTHERAPY

This approach uses both supportive and dynamic psychotherapeutic techniques. Depression is thought to arise in the context of relationships and emphasis is placed on understanding and improving the relationship skills of the patient. There is some evidence supporting the effectiveness of interpersonal psychotherapy in improving social functioning in patients who have recovered from symptoms of depression.

COGNITIVE THERAPY

Cognitive therapists help patients by focusing on their negative "cognitions" or thoughts about themselves, the present and the future. Negative thoughts about oneself lead to lowered self esteem; negative thoughts about the present lead to excessive caution and guardedness; and negative thoughts about the future lead to pessimism and hopelessness. Cognitive therapists believe that these negative thoughts can precipitate and perpetuate depression. Specific techniques of cognitive therapy have been worked out and a few studies have shown some effectiveness in treating depression.

BEHAVIOR THERAPY

Depressed patients have changes in their behaviors, and behavior therapy attempts to alleviate depression by returning behavior patterns toward normal. This approach helps patients increase the number of normal and nondepressed behaviors so that they will receive the positive reinforcements from thoughts and feelings associated with more normal behavior patterns. Evidence supporting the effectiveness of this approach is limited at present.

SUMMARY

Whatever else happens in psychotherapy, the patient is provided with a relationship with a doctor who has worked with other depressed patients. Through this relationship the therapist provides information about depression and support to the patient and his family. Psychotherapists also engender hope by providing an explanation for depression and help in pursuing a particular psychotherapeutic approach to relief of depression.

Psychotherapy is no longer the major treatment for

depression. While mild depression often disappears without treatment, it may stop sooner with psychotherapy.
Major and moderate depression usually require treatment
with antidepressant medications which are commonly
given in conjunction with psychotherapy.

ANTIDEPRESSANT MEDICATIONS

INTRODUCTION

Antidepressant medications have become the cornerstone of treatment of major depression and often have a role to play in the treatment of less severe depression. Indications for the use of antidepressant medications are usually straightforward and involve the presence of depressive mood, thoughts, behaviors and physical symptoms, as described on pages 1 to 3 and 24 to 28.

Sometimes depressions are hidden or "masked"—patients may complain of pain such as headache, backache or stomachache instead of sadness; or they may insist that they feel fine, but fail to go to work or look quite upset; or they may first notice panic or phobias (fears they recognize as unreasonable); or they may become obsessed with fears or pestered by compulsive rituals; or they may abuse alcohol or other drugs in attempts at self treatment of depression. Depression may also be signalled by other "atypical" physical or emotional complaints.

Clear diagnosis of depression or recognition of its possible presence are preliminary steps in the process of selecting appropriate medications or other treatments. A careful history, physical examination and any indicated laboratory tests are necessary to select the best treatment for depression. The physician should consider the patient's past history of depression and response to earlier treatments, family history of depression and any treatments found to be helpful, concurrent medical problems and their treatments, occupational and social impairment, severity of depression, risk of suicide, age, importance of speedy recovery, patient reliability and preference for treatment.

Several different classes of antidepressant medications are available and, in some classes, several different drugs have been shown to be effective. *Tricyclic* antidepressants and newer drugs of different chemical structure but similar effectiveness are the major antidepressant medications. *Monoamine oxidase inhibitors* (MAOIs) are the other main class of medications for treatment of depression. *Lithium*, used primarily in the treatment of mania and depression when those two disorders occur together or in sequence, may also be effective in cases where depression is the only problem. A number of *other medications* are sometimes added to the three main classes of medication (tricyclics, MAOIs and lithium). They will be discussed on pages 55 to 58.

Antidepressant medications are generally safe and effective when used as directed. But all medications are double-edged swords with unwanted side effects as well as the beneficial main effects for which they are given. Most antidepressant side effects are minor annoyances and many side effects decrease in severity as patients' bodies grow accustomed to the medication. When depression is treated with medications, there is almost always some minor cost in terms of side effects as well as the major benefit of relief of depression. Keeping the costs low and the benefits high is important and can almost always be accomplished in a cooperative relationship between patient and doctor.

Most major depressions will respond to treatment with the first antidepressant medication. If the first medication seems ineffective, it is important to make certain that it has been given in sufficient dose and for a sufficient period of time. Undertreatment is a common cause of treatment failure.

If a first medication fails, it is common practice to try a second medication unless there is reason to switch to electroconvulsive therapy for prompt relief of severe depression. Second medications may be of the same drug class or a shift may be made to another class of medications (for example, from tricyclics to MAOIs or lithium). If a second drug has failed to relieve depression (particularly if it is from a different class of antidepressant medications), combinations of antidepressants may be tried.

Depression which reaches psychotic proportions (when a person exhibits delusions or hallucinations and has clearly lost contact with reality) usually requires treatment with either electroconvulsive therapy (ECT) or an antidepressant medication plus an antipsychotic drug such as chlorpromazine (Thorazine), haloperidol (Haldol), or thiothixene (Navane).

TRICYCLIC, TETRACYCLIC, AND OTHER SIMILAR ANTIDEPRESSANTS

Tricyclic antidepressants are so named because their chemical compound includes three cyclic or ring structures. The first tricyclic, imipramine (Tofranil, Janimine, SK-Pramine), was introduced in 1958. Amitriptyline (Elavil, Endep, Amitid) was developed shortly after. Six other tricyclics have since been approved for antidepressant treatment and, recently, other antidepressant medications with tetracyclic (4 cyclic or ring structures) (maprotiline) and other chemical structures (trazodone) have appeared. Other antidepressant medications will be released for use in the United States in the next few years, and still others are available in other countries but not here.

There is little, if any, difference in *antidepressant effectiveness* among these drugs, although a particular individual may respond to one but not to another. There are differences in side effects which may suggest the use of one medication over another in a particular individual. Table 1 lists the commonly available tricyclic and similar antidepressant medicines and some of the *side effects* to be considered in their use.

Major side effects resulting from these medications fall into three general classes: *sedation* (drowsiness or sleepiness); *anticholinergic* (dry mouth, blurred vision, constipation, difficulty urinating and increased heart rate are the most common examples); and *orthostatic hypotension* (lightheadedness or dizziness when rising from a sitting or lying position). Table 1 lists the severity of these three classes of side effects.

These doses are rough guides. Smaller doses are sometimes effective, and larger doses are sometimes necessary. Flexibility is essential.

Less information is available regarding hypotensive side effects so we have chosen to use the terms "More" and "Less" rather than the "Low," "Medium" and "High" distinctions for other side effects.

Remember that most patients do well with medications listed as having High or More side effects. These relative side effect distinctions are presented to make it clear that if side effects are a problem, alternative medications are available.

Table 1—Common Antidepressant Medicines

Agent		Usual daily starting* dose (mg)	Usual effective daily dose* (mg)	Relative sedative effects	Relative anticho- linergic effects	Relative hypo- tensive effects
Generic name	Trade name					
Tricyclic antidepressants						
Amitriptyline	Endep Elavil Amitid	75	150-300	High	High	More
Amoxapine	Asendin	50 three times daily	150-400	Medium	Low	Less
Desipramine	Norpramin Pertofrane	50	100-300	Low	Low	More
Doxepin	Adapin Sinequan	75	75-300	High	Medium	More
Imipramine	Janimine SK-Pramine Tofranil	75	150-300	Medium	Medium	More
Nortriptyline	Aventyl Pamelor	50	50-100	Low	Medium	Less
Protriptyline	Vivactil	5 three times daily	15-60	Low	High	More
Trimipramine	Surmontil	75	50-200	High	Medium	More
Other antidepressants						
Maprotiline	Ludiomil	75	125-225	Medium	Low	Less
Trazodone	Desyrel	50 three times daily	150-400	High	Low	Less

*Lower doses (often ⅓ to ½ of the usual dose) are used with older patients.

Except for protriptyline, these medications are often taken in a single dose at bedtime. With this schedule, many side effects occur when the patient is asleep. If a single bedtime dose causes aftereffects such as sleepiness the next morning, the medication may be taken at dinner time or shortly thereafter. For some people, divided doses work best, even for medications that are usually given in a single dose. The doctor may prescribe a different schedule for taking the medication to try to find the best possible approach for any particular patient.

All of the antidepressant medications shown in Table 1 are effective in the same percentage of people. However, each individual may benefit from one antidepressant and not from another. Since it is presently impossible to predict which drug will help a particular person, minimizing side effects may be the determining factor in selecting the most appropriate drug.

SIDE EFFECTS

Individuals who must remain alert might be given an antidepressant with low sedative effect. Those who have trouble sleeping are often given a more sedating antidepressant to take at bedtime.

Older patients are more likely to be troubled with anticholinergic effects and may be given a medication less likely to cause anticholinergic problems. Main anticholinergic side effects are: dry mouth, palpitations (rapid and/or uneven heart beat), difficulty urinating, constipation and blurred vision.

Patients who experience lightheadedness or dizziness when arising from lying down or sitting positions might be given drugs low in hypotensive (low blood pressure) side effects.

Skin rash, weight gain or loss, restlessness, sweating, agitation, mild shaking (tremor), decreased sleep, and many other side effects can occur but do so infrequently. Any unusual experiences while taking an antidepressant medication should be reported to the physician.

For any given patient, other factors may dictate a choice of a drug which might seem likely to cause troublesome side effects. Since most patients have little difficulty with most side effects, medication side effects are usually not critical factors in drug selection. Physician familiarity with a particular medication and its side effects may be the single most important factor recommending its use. Few physicians can truly master the use of all antidepressant medications, and many wise physicians will stick with their familiar favorites unless their patients fail to improve.

QUESTIONS ABOUT TRICYCLIC
AND SIMILAR MEDICATIONS

(For convenience, we will refer to all the medications in Table 1 as "tricyclics.")

How long will it take to feel better? Tricyclic antidepressants do not work immediately. Several days or even several weeks pass before they become effective. It is unfortunate that the benefit is delayed because side effects often begin right away. It is important not to get discouraged and give up on the medication or take extra amounts of medication to try to get better faster.

Should I take tricyclic medication just when I feel depressed? NO! To be effective, tricyclics must be taken *regularly* until depression lifts, and then they are usually continued for three months to a year to prevent recurrence of depression. Depression usually begins to lift in 7 to 14 days — sometimes sooner, sometimes later.

People who feel less "depressed" right after they start taking an antidepressant are probably noticing the sedative side effect many of these medications have. Sedation can relieve anxiety, which is frequently part of depression.

How much medication will I take? There are general guidelines for effective doses (see Table 1) and your doctor will use them to begin treatment. However, people's bodies absorb, handle and excrete these drugs quite differently and two individuals given the same dose may have as much as a thirty-fold difference in blood level. Consequently different patients will be given different amounts of a drug to achieve the same benefit.

How does the doctor know the right amount of drug to give me? Aside from general guidelines, you and your doctor will monitor the symptoms and signs of depression for indications that the depression is beginning to lift. Sleep is often one of the first improvements patients notice, followed by improved appetite and later by reversal of pessimism and return of normal energy levels. Sometimes side effects become so severe that an adequate dose of a particular drug cannot be given. Then, switching to another drug is appropriate. Sometimes blood levels of antidepressant drugs are helpful in determining when an inadequate dose is being given.

How do tricyclics work? In depression, brain chemicals called "neurotransmitters" are thought to be reduced in amount. This causes reduced transmission of critical nerve impulses that has a final effect of causing depression. Although an oversimplification, tricyclic antidepressants may work by increasing the amount of essential neurotransmitters.

How can I deal with the dry mouth caused by the antidepressant? Dryness of the mouth is a common side effect of antidepressant medications, especially the tricyclics. This symptom is usually mild and tolerable and requires no treatment. If it becomes troublesome, however, a variety of measures may be helpful. They include sips of water, sugarless hard candy (such as lemon drops) and gum, and saliva-stimulating gum such as Quench. Candies and gums that contain sugar should be avoided and good oral hygiene by tooth brushing and flossing should be practiced. If dryness is especially severe, your doctor may prescribe a saliva substitute (Orex, Xero-Lube, Moi-Stir,

Salivant, VA Oralube, etc.), a saliva stimulating medication (pilocarpine) or switch you to a different antidepressant.

What can I do about the lightheaded feelings I get when I stand up? Lightheadedness or dizziness occurring on arising from lying down or sitting is usually due to a temporary fall in blood pressure which can be caused or aggravated by antidepressant drugs. If severe, this may result in loss of consciousness (blacking out), falls and, sometimes, injuries. Usually such symptoms, if they occur at all, are mild and can be prevented or relieved by getting up slowly — sitting for several seconds before standing rather than standing up quickly. It is also important to avoid becoming dehydrated (dried out) since this can make matters worse. Thus, proper attention to drinking adequate fluids is necessary. Finally, if symptoms persist (they usually improve over time) or if they are severe, contact your doctor since it may be necessary to adjust your medication or use other corrective measures.

What can I do if I feel sleepy? Sleepiness may diminish as your body grows accustomed to the tricyclic antidepressant. Your doctor may suggest taking the majority or all of the medication in the evening so that most of the sedative effect will occur while you are asleep. "Morning hangover" can often be decreased by taking the medication shortly after dinner rather than at bedtime. If drowsiness is a persistent problem, your doctor can switch to another antidepressant with less sedative effects. Caution should be exercised with regard to driving or operating machinery until sedative side effects have been resolved.

If we do switch medicines because of side effects, do I have to stop one before I can start another? The answer is no if you are switching between tricyclics or the other antidepressants found in Table 1. However, different doctors make the switch in different ways. Some stop one medicine, then begin the second right away or after a brief interval without medication. Some doctors decrease the dose of the first drug while increasing the dose of the second drug.

Lithium can be added to tricyclic and MAOI antidepressants, so no problem should arise if you are switched to lithium.

If you are changing to an MAOI, you may need to discontinue the tricyclic medication for two weeks *before* starting the MAOI. There are some exceptions to this rule but patients should *never* make this decision on their own because very serious elevations in blood pressure can result from improper combinations of tricyclics and MAOIs.

What's the difference between the generic and trade names of drugs? Generic names are the names given to chemical compounds. Trade names are used by drug companies to identify their particular brand of a generic drug. In soft drinks, "cola" is the generic name while "Coca Cola," "Pepsi Cola," and "Royal Crown Cola" are the trade names. Generic name drugs are often less expensive than trade name drugs. Although equivalent doses of generic drugs contain the same amount of antidepressant, they may differ in bio-availability (the amount of drug reaching the sites of action in the brain). Because of possible differences in bio-availability it may be best to continue with a single brand throughout a course of treatment.

MONOAMINE OXIDASE INHIBITOR ANTIDEPRESSANTS

MAOIs are thought to exert their antidepressant effect by slowing the breakdown of neurotransmitters, which are

Table 2—Monoamine Oxidase Inhibitors

Generic name	Trade name	Usual starting dose	Usual therapeutic daily dose
Isocarboxazid	Marplan	10 mg twice daily	30-40 mg
Phenelzine	Nardil	15 mg three times daily	60-90 mg
Tranylcypromine	Parnate	10 mg twice daily	30-60 mg

reduced in amount in people with depression. This explanation is an oversimplification, but it provides a rationale for the use of these medications which have been shown to be effective antidepressants.

There are three MAOIs currently available in the United States: isocarboxazid (Marplan), phenelzine (Nardil), and tranylcypromine (Parnate). Table 2 shows the usual starting and daily dose for adults.

In contrast to tricyclic antidepressants which are often given in a single dose at bedtime, MAOIs are usually taken in divided doses. The range of side effects for MAOIs is similar to the side effects found with tricyclic antidepressants with one important addition. MAOIs inhibit the oxidase enzyme which breaks down "monoamines" at many places in the body including the intestine. Consequently, people taking MAOIs may absorb more "monoamine" than usual.

Certain foods contain large amounts of tyramine, a monoamine which affects blood pressure. Large amounts of tyramine may lead to extreme elevations in blood pressure (a hypertensive reaction), sometimes to the point of breaking (rupturing) blood vessels and causing a stroke. Foods likely to cause this hypertensive reaction are listed in Table 3. Your doctor may provide a similar list. While most medications are compatible with MAOIs, those that are not can be quite dangerous.

Table 3
Substances Which Can Cause a Hypertensive
Reaction in Patients Taking an MAOI

Foods

Patients taking MAOIs must avoid:

Aged cheese in any form. Cottage and cream cheese are permitted
Yogurt
Marmite, Bovril, and similar concentrated yeast or meat extracts (beware of drinks and stews made with these products). Baked products raised with yeast are allowed.
Pickled herring
Liver
Alcohol in more than social (i.e., moderate) amounts (limit yourself to one glass of beer, wine, or sherry. Avoid Chianti wines altogether. You might take more if you are drinking only gin or vodka, but remember that one drink of alcohol may have a much greater effect when you are taking an MAOI)
Broad bean pods (limas, fava, Chinese, English, etc.) and banana skins
Canned figs
Food which is not fresh (or prepared from frozen or newly opened tinned food). Take special care to avoid pickled, fermented, smoked, or aged meat, fish, poultry, game, or offal.
Caffeine in large amounts (watch out for caffeine in cola)
Chocolate in large amounts
Any food which has given unpleasant symptoms previously

Some patients discover that they can consume small quantities of "forbidden" foods without having a hypertensive reaction. Before making any deviations from these dietary restrictions, you should discuss them with your doctor.

Medicines

While most medications are compatible with MAOIs, those that are not can be quite dangerous. Some medications in combination with MAOIs may cause hypertensive or other severe reactions. Consequently, patients taking MAOIs should not take *any* medicines, drugs, over-the-counter preparations (including cough and cold cures) or any other medication of any sort whatsoever without consulting their doctor. Make all doctors you see aware that you are taking an MAOI. Ordinary aspirin and acetaminophen (Tylenol is a common example) are all right if they are not part of a combination preparation for colds.

It is best for people taking MAOIs to avoid these foods and substances altogether, although some patients have used small amounts of some of these substances without experiencing a hypertensive reaction. However, the amount of potentially dangerous substances in foods can vary widely so what seemed safe at one time may cause problems at another.

Although the list of foods and drugs to avoid may seem quite long and complicated, most people usually have no difficulty following the instructions. The likelihood of a serious reaction is quite small.

MAOIs are a second line treatment for depression. They are seldom indicated as the first antidepressant medication for typical depression. Physicians might select them first for less typical depressions which are characterized by extreme anxiety, increased sleeping and/or appetite and loss of pleasure in most activities.

QUESTIONS ABOUT MAOIs

How would I know if I were having a hypertensive reaction? Mild hypertensive reactions may go unnoticed. Marked elevation in blood pressure may be signalled by headache at the back of the head, stiff neck, pounding heart beat and, less frequently, nausea, vomiting and dilated pupils.

What if I have a bad headache but no other symptoms? If the headache is of the kind and severity you often have (an "old friend"), you may decide to treat it with aspirin or acetaminophen (but not with combination cold remedies) and see how you feel. If the headache is atypical, or if your usual treatment is ineffective, you should contact your doctor or go to an emergency room for evaluation.

If I have a recognizable hypertensive reaction, what should I do? Go to your doctor's office or an emergency room where your blood pressure can be measured and, if found to be elevated, treatment can be given, usually with a drug called phentolamine (Regitine).

Is there anything I can do about hypertensive reactions if I can't get to an emergency room? If you were certain that you had a hypertensive reaction, you could take a pill containing phentolamine (Regitine) or chlorpromazine (Thorazine) that your doctor could give you to carry for this purpose. However, it's best to actually measure blood pressure before starting treatment, and it's best that such treatment be done under close observation by a physician. If you suspect a hypertensive reaction, you should certainly stop taking your MAOI medication and see your doctor to determine whether or not your blood pressure is increased. Appropriate corrective steps can then be taken.

LITHIUM

Lithium is often effective in controlling manic-depressive disorder (also called bipolar affective disorder) which is characterized by wide and often disabling mood swings. In manic-depressive disorder, mood can be elevated—with feelings of elation, expansiveness and euphoria—or depressed (see page 9). Lithium tends to stabilize mood at a more normal level.

Lithium also appears to be an effective antidepressant for some people who have only depression without ever experiencing any manic episodes with elevated mood.

Lithium treatment is preferred for many patients with manic-depressive disorder because of its effectiveness and because the side effects are generally fewer and less severe than those associated with other treatments for mania. However, lithium treatment is somewhat complicated and some physicians have not been trained in the use of lithium, which was first approved by the Food and Drug Administration in 1970. If your doctor prescribes lithium as a treatment for your depression, you should read *Lithium and Manic-Depression: A Guide* (see Suggested Reading).

COMBINATIONS OF ANTIDEPRESSANTS AND OTHER MEDICATIONS USED IN THE TREATMENT OF DEPRESSION

Combinations of tricyclics and MAOIs, tricyclics and lithium and MAOIs and lithium or all three medications are sometimes effective when single drugs have failed to help a patient.

Other medications are sometimes prescribed at the same time as tricyclics, MAOIs or lithium in an attempt to increase their antidepressant effect. These additional medications would not ordinarily be used if a satisfactory response is obtained with a tricyclic, MAOI or lithium alone. Among the medications shown to have some beneficial additive effect are thyroid hormone, L-tryptophan (an amino acid which is a building block for one neurotransmitter), vitamin B6 (also called pyridoxine) and, occasionally, stimulants such as amphetamine (Dexedrine) or methylphenidate (Ritalin).

QUESTIONS ABOUT OTHER MEDICATIONS

Why would other medications be helpful in some cases and not in others? There are many causes of depression. Each of these other medications treats different aspects of the several probable causes of depression. Thus, *thyroid hormone* deals with one aspect of a hormonal imbalance which may accompany severe depression. The goal in using *L-tryptophan* is to increase the amount of neurotransmitter by a different mechanism than the one involved in the use of tricyclics or MAOIs. While *vitamin B6* is rarely depleted, when vitamin B6 deficiency occurs, it is most often in women taking birth control pills (even though most women taking birth control pills have normal B6 levels). If B6 levels are low, they may need to be replenished before an antidepressant medication can be effective. The role of stimulants is controversial, in part because they have a clear potential for abuse. Nevertheless, they seem helpful for a few patients when used carefully for short periods of time.

Why not use a combination of medications all the time? Every medication has side effects and when more than one medication is used, it is likely that more side effects will occur. Also, certain combinations are potentially dangerous (combinations of MAOIs and stimulants, for example).

Finally, tricyclics, MAOIs or lithium alone are usually effective in treating depression so that combinations, with the added complications they produce, are seldom necessary.

What about combination drugs such as Limbitrol, Triavil and Etrafon? Limbitrol is a combination of the tricyclic antidepressant, amitriptyline, and a minor tranquilizer or anti-anxiety drug, chlordiazepoxide. Triavil and Etrafon combine amitriptyline and perphenazine, a major tranquilizer or antipsychotic drug. The idea behind these combinations is to provide some relief from anxiety, which is a prominent part of many depressions, with chlordiazepoxide or perphenazine while awaiting the antidepressant effect of the amitriptyline.

Proponents claim that these combinations permit a lower overall dose of amitriptyline and speedier symptomatic relief. Opponents point out that amitriptyline alone is as effective in the long run, that chlordiazepoxide has a slight dependency potential and perphenazine, while not causing dependency, can cause a disturbing disorder of abnormal movements called tardive dyskinesia. Any drug combination is inherently more complicated to use than single medications. Finally, amitriptyline, which is one of the more sedating tricyclic antidepressants, when combined with chlordiazepoxide or perphenazine, which also have some sedating properties, may prove too sedating for some patients.

What about alprazolam (Xanax) as an antidepressant? Alprazolam is an anti-anxiety drug or minor tranquilizer of the benzodiazepine family. Other drugs in the same class include chlordiazepoxide (Librium), clorazepate (Tranxene), diazepam (Valium), lorazepam (Ativan) and oxazepam (Serax).

As of January, 1984, alprazolam (Xanax) *has not been*

approved by the FDA for use in the treatment of depression, but some studies have shown it to have antidepressant properties as well as the anti-anxiety effect for which it is presently approved and prescribed. The dose of alprazolam required for antidepressant benefit may be higher than the effective anti-anxiety dose. This would tend to increase drowsiness, the main side effect of alprazolam. There is also a question about development of dependence to the benzodiazepine drugs, especially when taken for long periods and in large doses as might be needed for the treatment of depression. On the other hand, alprazolam is free from certain side effects that can be troublesome when conventional antidepressants are used (especially heart and autonomic). An effective antidepressant with such a side effect profile would be quite useful.

At present, the use of alprazolam (Xanax) in depression remains experimental and most doctors will not routinely use alprazolam for depression until further research has better defined its strengths and limitations.

ELECTROCONVULSIVE OR "SHOCK" THERAPY (ECT)

In the experience and judgment of many physicians (and patients with severe depressions who have received ECT and other antidepressant treatments), electroconvulsive therapy is the single most effective treatment for *severe* depression and has a number of advantages over other treatments.

ECT works rapidly so that patients can quickly return to productive living. It has a higher success rate for *severe* depression than any other single treatment approach.

ECT is clearly the treatment of choice when a person is making dangerous suicide attempts since attempts are exceedingly rare after a course of treatment has been started.

In psychotic depression where a person has lost contact with reality and has delusions or hallucinations (see page 2), ECT is more effective than antidepressant medications which must be used in *high doses* and often in combination with antipsychotic drugs to achieve a less prompt and effective result.

Patients in precarious medical condition usually tolerate ECT very well and with fewer complications than when treated with antidepressant drugs. Contrary to the common fears and dramatic misconceptions often associated with the terms "shock treatment" and "electroconvulsive therapy," the actual physiological stress and risk from the minimal electrical stimulus employed are very low. In the most severe cases of depression, ECT can be life saving. In one case, an 84-year-old woman with diabetes and heart failure was also severely depressed and highly agitated (physically overactive) because of her depression. The agitation aggravated her congestive heart failure and her life was in great jeopardy for this reason. Though in very poor physical condition, she tolerated and responded promptly to three electroconvulsive treatments on successive days. Relieved of her depression and constant agitation, she became compliant with her cardiac and diabetic treatments and progressed to recovery.

ECT is administered *after* the patient is put to sleep with a short acting anesthetic and *after* the patient's muscles are relaxed so that muscle contractions from the treatment will not damage muscles or bones. Patients do not remember or feel the treatment.

After most treatments, there is a brief period of confusion and memory loss for recent events. This usually lasts from 20 to 60 minutes. Temporary memory loss increases with the number and frequency of treatments but can be lessened by increasing the interval between treatments and by "unilateral" or one sided treatment. A new technique called brief-pulse ECT uses the minimum amount of electricity needed to produce an effective treatment and substantially reduces memory loss after each treatment and over a course of treatments.

Contrary to scare stories and subjective reports of lasting memory loss, repeated neuropsychological studies have failed to find any permanent effect on memory. In fact, memory is sometimes improved after ECT, probably because depression itself can have an adverse effect on memory. After the usual series of six to twelve treatments at intervals of two to three days, some decreasing memory loss may persist for as long as several months. Occasionally, patients complain of more persistent memory impairment which may not be apparent when tested objectively. Whether this is a reflection of insensitive testing procedures and/or whether this truly is a consequence of ECT continues to be investigated.

Once patients learn the great effectiveness and safety of ECT, they often prefer ECT to alternative treatments.

NEW AND LESS
FREQUENTLY USED
TREATMENTS

EXERCISE

Research over the past decade has shown that exercise has an antidepressant effect for many patients with mild to moderate depression. Exercise has not been shown to be of benefit in severe depression. No one is certain how exercise exerts its mood elevating effect. Some experts believe that simply moving large muscle masses in regular rhythmical ways is inconsistent with depression. Others maintain that exercise produces a fundamental alteration in brain chemistry, perhaps affecting neurotransmitters and endorphins (recently discovered naturally occurring morphine-like substances).

To be effective against depression, exercise must be done regularly at least three times and preferably five or more times per week for sessions lasting one half to one hour. In order to be able to carry on such an active program of exercise, the exercise must be comfortable, and it is here that problems often arise. Many people starting to exercise have in their mind's eye an image of the world's best athletes. This may lead them to push too hard, become sore, fatigued and possibly even injured. As a result, they understandably quit exercise before they have had a chance to obtain the benefits exercise can provide.

A combination of walking and running is the single most common form of exercise used for the treatment of depression. However, any regular aerobic exercise (done without building an oxygen debt — a simple test of aerobic exercise is the ability to whistle or carry on a conversation *while* exercising) program is likely to provide comparable benefits. Walking/running is the most practical approach to exercise for most people because it is inexpensive, requires no equipment beyond comfortable clothes and a good pair of shoes, is possible in all weather, and can be done alone or with others. Swimming, bicycling, rowing, and aerobic dance all have their advocates and devotees, but each requires facilities, equipment or companions that can interfere with the regular practice of exercise. Guides to using exercise for treating depression are found in Suggested Readings on page 79.

SLEEP DEPRIVATION

Recent studies have begun to confirm earlier case reports that some individuals with severe depression are transiently helped by remaining awake all night. A few individuals have been treated with this approach alone and are able to maintain a recovery from depression by continued judicious use of sleep deprivation.

The mechanism by which sleep deprivation alleviates depression is unclear. Some researchers feel that most depressed people have a phase shift in their basic circadian or 24-hour rhythms and that sleep deprivation helps correct this abnormality.

At this time, sleep deprivation is an experimental treatment and should not be used to the exclusion of other treatments which have been proven to be effective. Patients should not treat themselves with this experimental approach and only clinicians who are experienced in the use and effects of sleep deprivation should offer this treatment.

PSYCHOSURGERY

In rare cases of depression where all other treatments have failed, careful neurosurgical interruption of brain pathways has been shown to help about 50 percent of patients. The neurosurgical procedures are done under the control of exact three-dimensional measurements (stereotactic) so that the interruption of brain pathways is precisely defined and limited. The techniques are surprisingly safe and seldom cause complications in the form of personality change or epilepsy. Death as a result of this surgery is rare.

While clearly not to be undertaken lightly, psychosurgery has a place in the treatment of the most difficult cases of depression. We would never recommend psychosurgery until and unless other treatments had been given a full trial and found to be ineffective. In our hands, psychosurgery would never be recommended until two years had passed during which the full spectrum of alternative treatments had been tried and a spontaneous remission had failed to appear. Even then, we would recommend psychosurgery only for patients with severe depression which is causing extreme distress or disability.

SOME COMMON QUESTIONS ABOUT THE TREATMENT OF DEPRESSION

Who is the best professional to treat depression? Since primary care doctors (family or general practitioners or internists), psychiatrists (who are also physicians), and psychologists all treat depression, this is a common question and an understandable source of confusion.

Since most depressions requiring treatment usually respond to an antidepressant medication, a physician is the obvious first choice. Your primary care doctor already knows a great deal about your medical history, your family and other important aspects of your life. He or she is the best person to evaluate your depression and begin treatment if it is necessary. In most cases, this first treatment will be effective. If depression persists, your doctor knows the other doctors (psychiatrists or psychologists) who specialize in treating depression and will be able to make the most appropriate referral.

So, unless special circumstances exist (such as having worked with a depression specialist before or a suicide

67

attempt being the first warning of depression) we recommend that depression first be evaluated and treated by the primary care doctor who will arrange referral when necessary.

Which treatment is best for depression? Since depression is almost certainly caused by different factors, there is no single best treatment for depression. The best treatment for any individual's depression is the treatment which counteracts the causes of that particular depression. However, it is often impossible to pinpoint the causes of depression, so treatment is often begun on the basis of what is most often helpful for most depressions, which frequently means antidepressant medications.

Is taking antidepressants a sign of weakness? NO! Depression is a medical disorder, just as diabetes and pneumonia are medical disorders. People with depression need to take care of themselves and antidepressant medicines are just as important in the treatment of depression as insulin is in the treatment of diabetes.

If you are only working too hard or are unhappy because of a life situation that would make anyone unhappy, antidepressant medications will not provide you with energy or happiness. If physical pain is due to a problem other than depression, antidepressant medications will only rarely relieve the pain. Antidepressants work only when the medical disorder of depression is present. When depression is present, antidepressant medications usually give dramatic and gratifying relief from the symptoms of depression.

Which antidepressant am I likely to receive? If you have a common form of depression, then a tricyclic or one of the other antidepressants listed in Table 1 on page 45 will probably be prescribed, since they are presently the standard treatment for depression. New antidepressant drugs are being developed and some may be available by the time you read this book.

What if the first treatment doesn't work? Unfortunately, even the treatments most likely to be effective may not help a given individual. Fortunately, alternative treatments are likely to be helpful, and it is important to keep working with your physician until an effective treatment is found. If several treatments have not improved your condition, you and your doctor may benefit from a second opinion or consultation from another clinician.

Can I stop the antidepressant medicines as soon as I feel better? NO! It appears that antidepressants merely alleviate the symptoms of depression until the depression runs its course. Since depressions last from a few months to as long as two years if untreated, you would be likely to experience a relapse if you stop your antidepressant medicine. You and your doctor should work together on a plan, to discontinue your medication.

What happens if I forget to take my antidepressant medicine? If you are taking several doses each day and forget one, add it to your evening dose. If you take all of your medication in the evening, do not try to make up the missed dose the next morning but simply make certain that you take the correct dose the following evening and on subsequent evenings. Doubling your dose in a single day might cause annoying or dangerous side effects.

It is important to take antidepressant medications as prescribed and that means trying to take all of the medication at the correct time(s). Missing a single dose is unlikely to cause problems, but missing doses repeatedly could cause a return of depression.

How long do I have to take antidepressant medicine?
The length of treatment varies among individuals. Duration is determined by the frequency of depressive episodes and by how effective and tolerable the antidepressant treatment is for each person. Although continuous antidepressant treatment is helpful in certain cases, most people will not require it. The usual course of treatment runs from three months to one year. The best course of treatment for each person must be developed individually with his or her doctor. If a drug is not working despite an adequate dose, treatment for longer than 4 weeks is rarely indicated and an alternative drug should be used.

What about antidepressant drugs and pregnancy? Ideally, all medications should be avoided when a woman is trying to become pregnant and during the first three months of pregnancy. This approach will minimize the likelihood of a malformed baby. In some cases, however, a medication may be so necessary to a woman's health that it cannot be discontinued. Fortunately, there is no good evidence that the tricyclic or monoamine oxidase antidepressants are associated with a higher than normal incidence of malformations (lithium is somewhat riskier), and many women have had normal pregnancies and deliveries after taking these drugs throughout pregnancy. Since individual circumstances vary, prospective mothers taking antidepressants should discuss their medication and pregnancy with the doctor prior to conception if possible.

There are no known harmful effects from antidepressants on children whose fathers were taking antidepressants at the time of conception or whose mothers were taking antidepressants prior to but not during conception.

Antidepressant drugs are excreted in breast milk, and although the concentrations are quite low, a decision to breast feed should be made in consultation with the doctor.

Do depressed children need medicines? Doctors remain cautious about prescribing medications for children who are still growing and developing. While tricyclic antidepressants appear safe for children, concern remains about the possibility of unknown negative effects on their growth and development. On the other hand, depression itself can have devastating effects on a child's growth and development and occasionally leads to suicide, even in young children. Antidepressant medications are effective in treating depression in many children, but their use requires a full consideration of the possible risks and benefits.

Can older people take antidepressant medication? Depression in the elderly can be severe, debilitating, and deadly. Advanced age is no barrier to the successful treatment of depression. Because the elderly are likely to have associated medical illnesses, may be taking other medications, and are more sensitive to drug side effects, the use of antidepressant drugs can be more complicated than in younger persons. In general, lower doses of antidepressant may be necessary, more attention to the possibility of adverse interactions between drugs needed, and closer collaboration between treating physician and consultants required. In brief, antidepressant drugs can be used both effectively and safely in the elderly.

How will I feel while taking antidepressant medications? The main effect of antidepressants is to *lift or elevate mood* from a depressed level to a normal one. Once mood is returned to normal, antidepressants *stabilize* mood and usually prevent a return of depression as long as they continue to be taken. Some side effects are likely to occur. Side effects such as decreased worry or anxiety and increased sleep are quite welcome. Other side effects, while annoying, are usually tolerable and tend to lessen as time passes.

What if I am on a special diet? For *tricyclic antidepressants*, the only dietary caution is with the use of alcohol. The combination of tricyclics and alcohol is additive and a person taking tricyclics may find that a single drink has an effect equivalant to two or three drinks. Alcohol does *not* increase the effectiveness of antidepressant medications.

Monoamine oxidase inhibitors require several dietary precautions. Please see pages 52 and 53 for a list of foods and other substances that should be avoided.

In general, diets which do not markedly restrict salt or fluid intake should not interfere with *lithium* treatment.

Can I exercise while on antidepressant drug treatment? CERTAINLY! Exercise is an important factor in everyone's health, and has been shown to have antidepressant properties. Be sure to take in enough fluids and a normal amount of salt. (Salt pills are never needed.)

Is it dangerous to take other medications while on antidepressant medicines? Most medications may be combined with antidepressants. Some, however, may interact with them in such a way as to cause serious side effects. It's best to tell all doctors treating you that you are taking an antidepressant medication. Before taking any medication (prescription or non-prescription), ask your doctor or pharmacist whether it might interact adversely with your antidepressant.

What about blood levels of antidepressant medications? Blood levels of tricyclic antidepressant drugs can now be accurately measured and these measurements sometimes prove helpful in adjusting drug doses. However, blood tests are seldom needed with the tricyclic antidepressants (Table 1 on page 45). Blood levels of MAOIs (Table 2, page 51) are rarely obtained because direct assays are difficult to perform.

By contrast, determination of blood lithium levels is a simple, reliable laboratory procedure, essential to the proper management of lithium treatment.

Blood levels of tricyclics and MAOI blockade may be obtained to assist the physician in assessing the rate a given individual absorbs, metabolizes and excretes the drug. There is a thirty-fold difference in blood level with a given dose of tricyclic in different individuals. The usual clinical approach is to increase the dose until depression is relieved or side effects become too severe. Sometimes this results in a blood level too low (subtherapeutic) or too high (toxic). A few medications seem to have a "therapeutic window" of effective dose and blood level. Both beneath and above critical dosage and blood levels, the antidepressant effect is lost.

Lithium levels are obtained frequently when starting treatment and after any change in dose. It is *very important that blood levels be determined in the morning, as near as possible to twelve hours after the evening dose and before the morning dose.*

Are antidepressant medications addictive? *No!* They are not dope and if stopped, you would not have a craving for them. However, as with any medication which affects the central nervous system, it is wise to taper off the medication gradually so that your body can adjust to that change.

What if I need to see another doctor or have an operation while taking an antidepressant medication? When seeing other doctors or undergoing any medical or surgical procedure, always tell those involved that you are taking an antidepressant medication. This information should help insure that your antidepressant medication is managed safely and effectively. Do not assume that being on an antidepressant is only important to the doctor who prescribes it for you.

Are antidepressant medicines the best treatment for depression? For many people, yes. However, not everyone can tolerate antidepressant medications and not everyone is helped by them. Alternative treatment such as psychotherapy, electroconvulsive therapy, exercise, sleep deprivation and, rarely, psychosurgery, are available to help those who do not benefit from antidepressant medications. Despite their limitations, antidepressant medications have been of benefit to millions of individuals. Only you and your doctor can determine whether antidepressant medications will be the best treatment choice for you.

What about vitamins and minerals? There is no sound evidence that general vitamin or mineral supplements are useful in the treatment of depression. However, if a person chooses to take vitamin or mineral products as diet supplements, no adverse interactions with antidepressant medications would be expected. Infrequently, vitamin B6 deficiency may be a factor in causing depression, usually in women taking oral contraceptives. In this case, supplementation of vitamin B6 intake is important. Occasionally, other vitamin deficiencies can be associated with depression, as in vitamin B12 deficiency which can cause pernicious anemia.

Does it have to be either psychotherapy or medications? NO! All depressed patients need and can benefit from psychotherapy. But many patients with mild depression, most patients with moderate depression and all patients with severe depression need medications as well as psychotherapy for best results. Overall, medications are more effective than psychotherapy, particularly when depression is severe. And when depression is most severe, patients can seldom benefit from psychotherapy.

For moderate depression recent studies have shown that

a combination of antidepressant medications and psychotherapy is more helpful than either treatment alone.

Even though it is hard to show any direct benefit of
psychotherapy in severe depression and the effects of
psychotherapy may be weaker than medications in less
severe depression, psychotherapy does offer the understanding and support we all need in difficult times. It also
provides the physician with an opportunity to monitor the
patient's response to treatment with antidepressant medications.

After the worst of a depression is over, psychotherapy
may be helpful in identifying factors which have led to
depression and may help a person make changes that may
reduce the likelihood of subsequent depressions.

**If these antidepressant medications improve my mood,
aren't they like "pep pills" or "uppers" that people buy
on the streets?** ABSOLUTELY NOT! "Pep pills" or "uppers" give everybody a sudden burst of energy and distort
their sense of reality, whether they are depressed or not.
Pep pills and uppers are dangerous and addicting and are
used to treat depression only on rare occasions and then
only for short periods of time. Antidepressant medicines
do not change *an undepressed person's* mood and the only
effects a normal person is likely to experience are unwanted side effects such as dry mouth or sleepiness.

How safe are antidepressant medicines? Antidepressants are very safe when used as directed. Nevertheless,
any medication can cause problems and you will want to
follow your doctor's instructions closely to minimize the
possibility of difficulties. Excessive amounts of antidepressants (overdoses) can be quite dangerous.

**How bad are side effects from antidepressant medica-
tions?** Most people notice few side effects and find the

ones they do experience quite tolerable. Some patients have annoying side effects which make them "feel worse before they feel better." These side effects often decrease in severity as the body adjusts to the medication. A few people have such severe side effects that they must increase the dose very gradually or sometimes cannot take a particular medication at all.

Overall, many people notice some side effects but can continue the medication until they obtain the benefit of its main antidepressant effect.

Will antidepressant medicines affect my sex life? Sex drive is often reduced in depression and antidepressant medications usually restore sex drive to a normal level. If sex drive has continued at a normal level in spite of depression, antidepressant medications usually have little effect on it. Infrequently, antidepressant medications can lower sex drive or even cause temporary impotence in males or loss of orgasm in females, which is relieved by stopping or changing medications.

What if side effects from medications are severe? Most side effects are most troublesome at the beginning of treatment and then diminish in severity. If your side effects are particularly severe, it is best to hold the next dose of medication and talk about the side effects with your doctor rather than making a change on your own. Sometimes simple adjustments in the dose or the schedule for taking the antidepressant medication will minimize side effects. At other times a change to another antidepressant may be helpful.

Are there any long-term side effects of antidepressant medicines? Most people suffering from depression take antidepressant medicines for periods of a few months to a few years. However, all antidepressant medications (tricyclics, MAOIs and lithium) have been used continuously for many years without producing noticeable long-term side effects.

Lithium is something of a special case since it has been shown to cause underactivity of the thyroid gland (hypothyroidism) and reduction in kidney function in a few patients. Both of these conditions can be identified by routine laboratory tests and are usually corrected by simple measures.

Although long-term effects are either unknown or unrecognized (tricyclics and MAOIs) or easily identified so they can be dealt with before they become serious (lithium), physicians remain concerned about possible long-term side effects that might emerge very late in the course of treating depression with medications. Consequently, most physicians will talk with their patients about the relative risks of stopping medication (a new episode of depression might occur) versus the small or unknown risk of some late developing side effect. Physicians also evaluate their patients periodically for new side effects that may be caused by continued use of medication.

Are antidepressant medications used for anything other than depression? Sometimes antidepressants are tried for migraine headache or other kinds of pain that fail to respond to conventional treatments. Bedwetting is sometimes treated with antidepressants. Panic attacks and obsessive-compulsive disorder are also treated with antidepressants in combination with behavioral psychotherapies. When antidepressants are helpful, it may be unclear whether the antidepressant has an effect on the surface complaint (pain, panic, obsessions and compulsions) or whether the drug is treating an underlying depression. These disorders may fall into the category of "masked" depressions (see page 41).

How can someone learn all that is important about depression and its treatments? A book of this size cannot provide answers to every question that might be asked about depression. The material included here was selected because doctors and patients thought it was especially important.

The following suggestions may help you learn more about depression and the different ways of treating it:

Read this book and be sure to note any areas where you have questions.

Ask your doctor these questions and any others you might have.

Re-read the book from time to time to refresh your memory. Share it with close friends and family members and discuss areas that are particularly important to you.

Refer to the readings suggested below.

There are self-help groups around the country which offer support and information to people with depression. Contact the Center For Affective Disorders (see page 81) to find out if there is such a program in your area. There is no charge for this service.

SUGGESTED READINGS (prices as of August, 1983)

The following books may be helpful in better understanding depression, manic-depression, lithium, and mental illness:

Non-technical

A Season in Hell - Percy Knauth. Harper and Row, New York, 1975. $7.95

Depression, The Facts - George Winokur. Oxford University Press, New York. $12.95

Feeling Good: The New Mood Therapy - David Burns. Signet, New York, 1980. $12.95

From Sad to Glad - Nathan S. Kline. Putnam, New York, 1974. $7.95

Genes and the Mind, Inheritance of Mental Illness - Ming T. Tsuang and R. Vandermey. Oxford University Press, New York, 1980. $12.95

Holiday of Darkness - Norman S. Endler. John Wiley and Sons, Inc., New York, 1982. $15.95

How to Control Your Depression - Peter Lewinsohn, Ricardo Munoz, Mary Ann Youngren, and Antonette Zeiss. Prentice Hall, Englewood Cliffs, NJ, 1978. $8.95

Lithium and Manic Depression: A Guide. Lithium Information Center, Madison, WI, 1982. $3.00

Mind, Mood, and Medicine - Paul H. Wender and Donald F. Klein. Farrar, Straus & Giroux, New York, 1981. $15.95

Moodswing: The Third Revolution in Psychiatry - Ronald Fieve. William Morrow, New York, 1975. $8.95

Psychiatry: A Personal View - Milton H. Miller. Charles Scribner's Sons, New York, 1983. $15.95

Running Guides - Roger R. Eischens and John H. Greist. Center For Affective Disorders, Madison, WI. $3.00

Your Brother's Keeper: A Guide for Families of the Mentally Ill - James R. Morrison. Nelson-Hall, Chicago, 1981. $20.95

Technical

Antidepressant Treatment: The Essentials - John H. Greist and Thomas H. Greist. Williams and Wilkins, Baltimore, 1979. $9.95

Cognitive Therapy of Depression - Aaron T. Beck, John T. Rush, Brian Shaw, and Gary Emery. Guilford Press, New York, 1979. $22.50

Diagnosis and Drug Treatment of Psychiatric Disorders: Adults and Children - Donald F. Klein, Rachel Gittelman, Frederic V. Quitkin, and Arthur Rifkin. Williams and Wilkins, Second Edition, Baltimore, 1980. $42.00

Electroconvulsive Therapy - Task Force Report 14, American Psychiatric Association, Washington, DC, 1978. $12.00

Lithium Encyclopedia for Clinical Practice - James W. Jefferson, John H. Greist, and Deborah L. Ackerman. American Psychiatric Press, Washington, DC, 1983. $19.50

Treatment of Mental Disorders - Edited by John H. Greist, James W. Jefferson, and Robert L. Spitzer. Oxford University Press, New York, 1982. $19.00

We hope to revise and update this book from time to time. Your comments, suggestions and criticisms are most welcome. Please contact:

CENTER FOR AFFECTIVE DISORDERS
Department of Psychiatry
University of Wisconsin
Center for Health Sciences
600 Highland Avenue
Madison, Wisconsin 53792
USA

Telephone (608) 263-6129

SUMMING UP

Depression is a common disorder and major depression affects at least 10 percent of the population at some time during their lifetime. Even larger percentages suffer from mild or moderate depression and at any one point in time, 5 percent of the population is experiencing depression severe enough to need treatment.

Depression can be very severe. People who have suffered both major depression and a serious medical illness such as heart attack usually say that depression was by far the worse experience. While medical problems are usually confined to one organ system (such as the heart and blood vessels—"cardiovascular system"), depression affects many organ systems (stomach and intestines, endocrine or hormonal, nervous, etc.) and the person's thinking, feelings and behavior. The most extreme behavioral abnormality is suicide which indicates the deep and pervasive pain depressed people can feel.

While depression is usually easy to diagnose once it is

considered, it is often unrecognized, confused with fatigue or frustration and may be "masked" or hidden, appearing as physical complaints such as pain or psychological changes such as withdrawal, irritability or anxiety.

Depression tends to run in families and to reoccur. The causes of depression are presently unknown in most cases. Improper functioning of brain chemicals (neurotransmitters) is thought to be involved in most depression. Occasionally, depression is caused by a medical illness (page 8) or alcohol or medications (page 17).

Recognition and diagnosis of depression are crucial first steps to recovery. Since many patients go to their general physician with complaints of fatigue, pain, irritability or anxiety as well as frank depression, general physicians provide effective first-line diagnosis and treatment of depression. Psychiatrists, psychologists and other mental health clinicians with special expertise and extensive experience in treating depression are often consulted by general physicians when routine treatments are ineffective. Some patients contact mental health clinicians directly for diagnosis and treatment of depression.

Antidepressant medications are the cornerstone of treatment for major depression and also have an important role to play in the treatment of moderate and even mild depression. Most patients can take antidepressant medication safely and with only minimal side effects to achieve a rapid recovery from depression. The antidepressant medications stand in a class by themselves and are not sedatives, "downers," "uppers" or "dope." They are not addicting.

Psychotherapy is also used to treat depression. Present evidence indicates that a combination of antidepressant medication and psychotherapy is the best treatment for most depressions.

Where basic treatments are ineffective, combinations of

two or more medications or electroconvulsive therapy are often helpful.

Depression can have a devastating effect on patients and their families. Fortunately, helpful treatment is available and most patients recover promptly and return to full functioning. The most difficult step to recovery from depression is the first one — recognizing that depression is a possibility and that recovery is highly likely if diagnosis and treatment are sought.

APPENDIX

The material in this Appendix has been excerpted from the *Diagnostic and Statistical Manual of Mental Disorders*, Third Edition (DSM-III), published in 1980 by the American Psychiatric Association, 1400 K Street, N.W., Washington, DC 20005.

Affective Disorders*

The essential feature of this group of disorders is a disturbance of mood, accompanied by a full or partial manic or depressive syndrome, that is not due to any other physical or mental disorder. Mood refers to a prolonged emotion that colors the whole psychic life; it generally involves either depression or elation. The manic and depressive syndromes each consist of characteristic symptoms that tend to occur together.

In other classifications these disorders are grouped in various categories, including Affective, Personality, and Neurotic Disorders.

Subclassification of Affective Disorders. The classification of Affective Disorders in DSM-III differs from many other classifications based on such dichotomous distinctions as neurotic vs. psychotic or endogenous vs. reactive.

In this manual the class Affective Disorders is divided into Major Affective Disorders, in which there is a full affective syndrome; Other Specific Affective Disorders, in which there is only a partial affective syndrome of at least two years' duration; and finally, Atypical Affective Disorders, a category for those affective disorders that cannot be classified in either of the two specific subclasses.

Major Affective Disorders include Bipolar Disorder and Major Depression, which are distinguished by whether or not there has ever been a manic episode. A category of Manic Disorder is not included in this classification; instead, when there has been one or more manic episodes, with or without a history of a major depressive episode, the category Bipolar Disorder is used. Bipolar Disorder is subclassified at the fourth digit as Mixed, Manic, or Depressed; Major Depression is subclassified at the fourth digit as Single Episode or Recurrent. The current episode is further subclassified at the fifth digit to reflect certain characteristics such as the presence of psychotic features and, in the case of a major depressive episode, the presence of Melancholia.†

Other Specific Affective Disorders include Cyclothymic Disorder and Dysthymic Disorder. In Cyclothymic Disorder there are symptoms characteristic of both the depressive and the manic syndromes, but they are not of sufficient severity and duration to meet the criteria for major depressive or manic episodes. In Dysthymic Disorder the symptoms are not of sufficient severity and duration

---

* The proper descriptive term for this group of disorders should be "Mood Disorders"; however, common usage and historical continuity favor retention of the term "Affective Disorders."

† A term from the past, in this manual used to indicate a typically severe form of depression that is particularly responsive to somatic therapy. The clinical features that characterize this syndrome have been referred to as "endogenous." Since the term "endogenous" implies, to many, the absence of precipitating stress, a characteristic not always associated with this syndrome, the term "endogenous" is not used in DSM-III.

to meet the criteria for a major depressive episode, and there have been no hypomanic periods. A theoretically possible third disorder in this group is Chronic Hypomanic Disorder, which would require hypomanic features of at least two years' duration, but not depressive periods; the existence of such a syndrome has not been well enough established to warrant inclusion as a distinct disorder. These chronic disorders may have a superimposed episode of Major Affective Disorder, in which case both diagnoses should be recorded.

MAJOR AFFECTIVE DISORDERS*

The essential feature is an illness involving either a manic episode (see below) or a major depressive episode (p. 210). These major affective episodes are not diagnosed if the affective disturbance is due to an Organic Mental Disorder or if it is superimposed on Schizophrenia.

Manic Episode

The essential feature is a distinct period when the predominant mood is either elevated, expansive, or irritable and when there are associated symptoms of the manic syndrome. These symptoms include hyperactivity, pressure of speech, flight of ideas, inflated self-esteem, decreased need for sleep, distractibility, and excessive involvement in activities that have a high potential for painful consequences, which is not recognized.

The elevated mood may be described as euphoric, unusually good, cheerful, or high; often has an infectious quality for the uninvolved observer; but is recognized as excessive by those who know the individual well. The expansive quality of the mood disturbance is characterized by unceasing and unselective enthusiasm for interacting with people and seeking involvement with other aspects of the environment. Although elevated mood is considered the prototypical symptom, the predominant mood disturbance may be irritability, which may be most apparent when the individual is thwarted.

The hyperactivity often involves excessive planning of and participation in multiple activities (e.g., sexual, occupational, political, religious). Almost invariably there is increased sociability, which includes efforts to renew old acquaintanceships and calling friends at all hours of the night. The intrusive, domineering, and demanding nature of these interactions is not recognized by the individual. Frequently, expansiveness, unwarranted optimism, grandiosity, and lack of judgment lead to such activities as buying sprees, reckless driving, foolish business investments, and sexual behavior unusual for the individual. Often the activities have a disorganized, flamboyant, or bizarre quality, for example, dressing in colorful or strange garments, wearing excessive, poorly applied make-up, or distributing candy, money, or advice to passing strangers.

Manic speech is typically loud, rapid, and difficult to interrupt. Often it is

---

* The organization of the text for the Major Affective Disorders departs from the usual method of presentation in order to avoid redundancy. The essential features, associated features, differential diagnosis and diagnostic criteria of manic and major depressive episodes are described first. Age at onset, course and other features of both manic and major depressive episodes are discussed next. Finally, the diagnostic criteria for the specific Major Affective Disorders are listed.

full of jokes, puns, plays on words, and amusing irrelevancies. It may become theatrical, with dramatic mannerisms and singing. Sounds rather than meaningful conceptual relationships may govern word choice (clanging). If the mood is more irritable than expansive, there may be complaints, hostile comments, and angry tirades.

Frequently there is flight of ideas, i.e., a nearly continuous flow of accelerated speech with abrupt changes from topic to topic, usually based on understandable associations, distracting stimuli, or plays on words. When flight of ideas is severe, the speech may be disorganized and incoherent. However, loosening of associations and incoherence may occur even when there is no flight of ideas, particularly if the individual is on medication.

Distractibility is usually present and manifests itself as rapid changes in speech or activity as a result of responding to various irrelevant external stimuli, such as background noise or signs or pictures on the wall.

Characteristically, there is inflated self-esteem, ranging from uncritical self-confidence to marked grandiosity, which may be delusional. For instance, advice may be given on matters about which the individual has no special knowledge, such as how to run a mental hospital or the United Nations. Despite a lack of any particular talent, a novel may be started, music composed, or publicity sought for some impractical invention. Grandiose delusions involving a special relationship to God or some well-known figure from the political, religious, or entertainment world are common.

Almost invariably there is a decreased need for sleep; the individual awakens several hours before the usual time, full of energy. When the sleep disturbance is severe, the individual may go for days without any sleep at all and yet not feel tired.

The term "hypomania" is used to describe a clinical syndrome that is similar to, but not as severe as, that described by the term "mania" or "manic episode."

Associated features. A common associated feature is lability of mood, with rapid shifts to anger or depression. The depression, expressed by tearfulness, suicidal threats, or other depressive symptoms, may last moments, hours, or, more rarely, days. Occasionally the depressive and manic symptoms intermingle, occurring at the same time; or they may alternate rapidly within a few days. Less often, in Bipolar Disorder, Mixed, the depressive symptoms are more prominent and last at least a full day, and there is the full symptom picture of manic and major depressive episodes.

When delusions or hallucinations are present, their content is usually clearly consistent with the predominant mood (mood-congruent). God's voice may be heard explaining that the individual has a special mission. Persecutory delusions may be based on the idea that the individual is being persecuted because of some special relationship or attribute. Less commonly, the content of the hallucinations or delusions has no apparent relationship to the predominant mood (mood-incongruent). The usefulness of the distinction between mood-congruent and mood-incongruent psychotic features is controversial.

Differential diagnosis of manic episode. **Organic Affective Syndromes** with mania may be due to such substances as amphetamines or steroids, or to some other known organic factor, such as multiple sclerosis. The diagnosis of a manic episode should be made only if a known organic etiology can be excluded. For further discussion, see p. 117.

In **Schizophrenia, Paranoid Type**, there may be irritability and anger that are difficult to distinguish from similar features in a manic episode. In such instances it may be necessary to rely on features that, on a statistical basis, are associated differentially with the two conditions. For example, the diagnosis of a manic episode is more likely if there is a family history of Affective Disorder, good premorbid adjustment, and a previous episode of an Affective Disorder from which there was complete recovery.

The diagnosis **Schizoaffective Disorder** may be made whenever the clinician is unable to make a differential diagnosis between manic episode and Schizophrenia. Although no criteria for Schizoaffective Disorder are provided in this manual, several examples of clinical situations in which this diagnosis might be appropriate are given on p. 202.

In **Cyclothymic Disorder** there are hypomanic periods, but the full manic syndrome is not present. However, in some instances a manic episode may be superimposed on Cyclothymic Disorder. In such cases both Bipolar Disorder and Cyclothymic Disorder should be diagnosed, since it is likely that when the individual recovers from the manic episode, the Cyclothymic Disorder will persist.

Diagnostic criteria for a manic episode

A. One or more distinct periods with a predominantly elevated, expansive, or irritable mood. The elevated or irritable mood must be a prominent part of the illness and relatively persistent, although it may alternate or intermingle with depressive mood.

B. Duration of at least one week (or any duration if hospitalization is necessary), during which, for most of the time, at least three of the following symptoms have persisted (four if the mood is only irritable) and have been present to a significant degree:

    (1) increase in activity (either socially, at work, or sexually) or physical restlessness

    (2) more talkative than usual or pressure to keep talking

    (3) flight of ideas or subjective experience that thoughts are racing

    (4) inflated self-esteem (grandiosity, which may be delusional)

    (5) decreased need for sleep

    (6) distractibility, i.e., attention is too easily drawn to unimportant or irrelevant external stimuli

    (7) excessive involvement in activities that have a high potential for painful consequences which is not recognized, e.g., buying sprees, sexual indiscretions, foolish business investments, reckless driving

C. Neither of the following dominate the clinical picture when an affective syndrome (i.e., criteria A and B above) is not present, that is, before it developed or after it has remitted:

(1) preoccupation with a mood-incongruent delusion or hallucination (see definition below)
(2) bizarre behavior

D. Not superimposed on either Schizophrenia, Schizophreniform Disorder, or a Paranoid Disorder.

E. Not due to any Organic Mental Disorder, such as Substance Intoxication.

(**Note:** A hypomanic episode is a pathological disturbance similar to, but not as severe as, a manic episode. See Atypical Bipolar Disorder, p. 223.)

Fifth-digit code numbers and criteria for subclassification of manic episode
6— In Remission. This fifth-digit category should be used when in the past the individual met the full criteria for a manic episode but now is essentially free of manic symptoms or has some signs of the disorder but does not meet the full criteria. The differentiation of this diagnosis from no mental disorder requires consideration of the period of time since the last episode, the number of previous episodes, and the need for continued evaluation or prophylactic treatment.

4— With Psychotic Features. This fifth-digit category should be used when there apparently is gross impairment in reality testing, as when there are delusions or hallucinations or grossly bizarre behavior. When possible, specify whether the psychotic features are mood-incongruent. (The non-ICD-9-CM fifth-digit 7 may be used instead to indicate that the psychotic features are mood-incongruent; otherwise, mood-congruence may be assumed.)

Mood-congruent Psychotic Features: Delusions or hallucinations whose content is entirely consistent with the themes of inflated worth, power, knowledge, identity, or special relationship to a diety or famous person; flight of ideas without apparent awareness by the individual that the speech is not understandable.

Mood-incongruent Psychotic Features: Either (a) or (b):
(a) Delusions or hallucinations whose content does not involve themes of either inflated worth, power, knowledge, identity, or special relationship to a deity or famous person. Included are such symptoms as persecutory delusions, thought insertion, and delusions of being controlled, whose content has no apparent relationship to any of the themes noted above.

(b) Any of the following catatonic symptoms: stupor, mutism, nega-
tivism, posturing.

2– **Without Psychotic Features.** Meets the criteria for manic episode,
but no psychotic features are present.

0– **Unspecified.**

Major Depressive Episode

The essential feature is either a dysphoric mood, usually depression, or loss of
interest or pleasure in all or almost all usual activities and pastimes. This
disturbance is prominent, relatively persistent, and associated with other symptoms of the depressive syndrome. These symptoms include appetite disturbance,
change in weight, sleep disturbance, psychomotor agitation or retardation,
decreased energy, feelings of worthlessness or guilt, difficulty concentrating or
thinking, and thoughts of death or suicide or suicidal attempts.

An individual with a depressive syndrome will usually describe his or her
mood as depressed, sad, hopeless, discouraged, down in the dumps, or in terms
of some other colloquial variant. Sometimes, however, the mood disturbance
may not be expressed as a synonym for depressive mood but rather as a
complaint of "not caring anymore," or as a painful inability to experience
pleasure. In a child with a depressive syndrome there may not be complaints
of any dysphoric mood, but its existence may be inferred from a persistently
sad facial expression.

Loss of interest or pleasure is probably always present in a major depressive episode to some degree, but the individual may not complain of this or
even be aware of the loss, although family members may notice it. Withdrawal
from friends and family and neglect of avocations that were previously a
source of pleasure are common.

Appetite is frequently disturbed, usually with loss of appetite, but occasionally with increased appetite. When loss of appetite is severe, there may be
significant weight loss or, in the case of children, failure to make expected
weight gains. When appetite is markedly increased there may be significant
weight gain.

Sleep is commonly disturbed, more frequently with insomnia present, but
sometimes with hypersomnia. The insomnia may involve difficulty falling asleep
(initial insomnia), waking up during sleep and then returning to sleep only with
difficulty (middle insomnia), or early morning awakening (terminal insomnia).

Psychomotor agitation takes the form of inability to sit still, pacing, hand-
wringing, pulling or rubbing of hair, skin, clothing, or other objects, outbursts
of complaining or shouting, or pressure of speech. Psychomotor retardation may
take the form of slowed speech, increased pauses before answering, low or
monotonous speech, slowed body movements, a markedly decreased amount of
speech (poverty of speech), or muteness. (In children there may be hypoactivity
rather than psychomotor retardation.) A decrease in energy level is almost

invariably present, and is experienced as sustained fatigue even in the absence of physical exertion. The smallest task may seem difficult or impossible to accomplish.

The sense of worthlessness varies from feelings of inadequacy to completely unrealistic negative evaluations of one's worth. The individual may reproach himself or herself for minor failings that are exaggerated and search the environment for cues confirming the negative self-evaluation. Guilt may be expressed as an excessive reaction to either current or past failings or as exaggerated responsibility for some untoward or tragic event. The sense of worthlessness or guilt may be of delusional proportions.

Difficulty in concentrating, slowed thinking, and indecisiveness are frequent. The individual may complain of memory difficulty and appear easily distracted.

Thoughts of death or suicide are common. There may be fear of dying, the belief that the individual or others would be better off dead, wishes to die, or suicidal plans or attempts.

Associated features. Common associated features include depressed appearance, tearfulness, feelings of anxiety, irritability, fear, brooding, excessive concern with physical health, panic attacks, and phobias.

When delusions or hallucinations are present, their content is usually clearly consistent with the predominant mood (mood-congruent). A common delusion is that one is being persecuted because of sinfulness or some inadequacy. There may be nihilistic delusions of world or personal destruction, somatic delusions of cancer or other serious illness, or delusions of poverty. Hallucinations, when present, are usually transient and not elaborate, and may involve voices that berate the individual for his or her shortcomings or sins.

Less commonly the content of the hallucinations or delusions has no apparent relationship to the mood disturbance (mood-incongruent). This is particularly the case with persecutory delusions, in which the individual may be at a loss to explain why he or she should be the object of persecution. The usefulness of the distinction between mood-congruent and mood-incongruent psychotic features is controversial.

Age-specific associated features. Although the essential features of a major depressive episode are similar in infants, children, adolescents, and adults, there are differences in the associated features.

In prepubertal children separation anxiety may develop and cause the child to cling, to refuse to go to school, and to fear that he or she or the parents will die. A previous history of separation anxiety may result in more intense anxiety symptoms with the onset of a major depressive episode.

In adolescent boys negativistic or frankly antisocial behavior may appear. Feelings of wanting to leave home or of not being understood and approved of, restlessness, grouchiness, and aggression are common. Sulkiness, a reluctance to cooperate in family ventures, and withdrawal from social activities, with retreat to one's room, are frequent. School difficulties are likely. There may be inattention to personal appearance and increased emotionality, with particular sensitivity to rejection in love relationships. Substance Abuse may develop.

In elderly adults there may be symptoms suggesting Dementia, such as disorientation, memory loss, and distractibility. Loss of interest or pleasure in the individual's usual activities may appear as apathy; difficulty in concentration as inattentiveness. These symptoms make the differential diagnosis of "pseudo-dementia" (due to depression) from true Dementia (an Organic Mental Disorder) particularly difficult (p. 111).

Differential diagnosis of major depressive episode. An **Organic Affective Syndrome with depression** may be due to substances such as reserpine, to infectious diseases such as influenza, or to hypothyroidism. Only by excluding organic etiology can one make the diagnosis of a major depressive episode. For further discussion, see p. 117.

Primary Degenerative Dementia or **Multi-infarct Dementia**, because of the presence of disorientation, apathy, and complaints of difficulty concentrating or of memory loss, may be difficult to distinguish from a major depressive episode occurring in the elderly. If the features suggesting a major depressive episode are at least as prominent as those suggesting Dementia, it is best to diagnose a major depressive episode and assume that the features suggesting Dementia represent a pseudo-dementia that is a manifestation of the major depressive episode. In such cases the successful treatment of the major depressive episode often results in the disappearance of the symptoms suggesting Dementia. If the features suggesting Dementia are more prominent than the depressive features, the diagnosis should be the appropriate form of Dementia, but the presence of depressive features should be noted.

If a **psychological reaction to the functional impairment associated with a physical illness** that does not involve the central nervous system causes a depression that meets the full criteria for a major depressive episode, the Major Depression should be recorded on Axis I, the physical disorder on Axis III, and the severity of the psychosocial stressor on Axis IV. Examples would include the psychological reaction to the amputation of a leg or to the development of a life-threatening or incapacitating illness.

In **Schizophrenia** there is usually considerable depressive symptomatology. If an episode of depression follows an episode of Schizophrenia and is superimposed upon the residual phase of Schizophrenia, the additional diagnosis of either Atypical Depression or Adjustment Disorder with Depressed Mood may be made, but not Major Depression. An individual with a major depressive episode may have psychotic symptoms; however, the diagnosis of Schizophrenia is made in the presence of a full depressive syndrome only if the affective symptoms follow the psychotic symptoms or are brief relative to the duration of the psychotic symptoms. An individual with Schizophrenia, Catatonic Type, may appear to be withdrawn and depressed, and it may be difficult to distinguish this condition from Major Depression with psychomotor retardation. In such instances it may be necessary to rely on features that on a statistical basis are associated differentially with the two disorders. For example, the diagnosis of a major depressive episode is more likely if there is a family history of Affective Disorder, good premorbid adjustment, and a previous episode of affective disturbance from which there was complete recovery.

The diagnosis of **Schizoaffective Disorder** can be made whenever the clinician is unable to make a differential diagnosis between a major depressive episode and Schizophrenia. Although no criteria for Schizoaffective Disorder are provided in this manual, several examples of clinical situations in which this diagnosis might be appropriate are given on p. 202.

In **Dysthymic** and **Cyclothymic Disorders** there are features of the depressive syndrome, but they are not of sufficient severity and duration to meet the criteria for a major depressive episode. However, in some instances, a major depressive episode is superimposed on one of these disorders. In such cases both diagnoses should be recorded, since it is likely that after recovering from the major depressive episode, either a Dysthymic or a Cyclothymic Disorder will persist.

Chronic mental disorders, such as **Obsessive Compulsive Disorder** or **Alcohol Dependence,** when associated with depressive symptoms, may suggest a Major Depression. The additional diagnosis of Major Depression should be made only if the full depressive syndrome is present and persistent. In such instances both the chronic mental disorder and the superimposed Major Depression should be recorded.

In **Separation Anxiety Disorder,** depressive symptoms are common, but if the full depressive syndrome is not present, only Separation Anxiety Disorder should be diagnosed. On the other hand, children with Separation Anxiety Disorder may develop a superimposed major depressive episode, in which case both diagnoses should be made.

Uncomplicated Bereavement is distinguished from a major depressive episode and is not considered a mental disorder even when associated with the full depressive syndrome (see p. 333). However, if bereavement is unduly severe or prolonged, the diagnosis may be changed to Major Depression.

Diagnostic criteria for major depressive episode
A. Dysphoric mood or loss of interest or pleasure in all or almost all usual activities and pastimes. The dysphoric mood is characterized by symptoms such as the following: depressed, sad, blue, hopeless, low, down in the dumps, irritable. The mood disturbance must be prominent and relatively persistent, but not necessarily the most dominant symptom, and does not include momentary shifts from one dysphoric mood to another dysphoric mood, e.g., anxiety to depression to anger, such as are seen in states of acute psychotic turmoil. (For children under six, dysphoric mood may have to be inferred from a persistently sad facial expression.)

B. At least four of the following symptoms have each been present nearly every day for a period of at least two weeks (in children under six, at least three of the first four).

(1) poor appetite or significant weight loss (when not dieting) or increased appetite or significant weight gain (in children under six, consider failure to make expected weight gains)

(2) insomnia or hypersomnia

(3) psychomotor agitation or retardation (but not merely subjective feelings of restlessness or being slowed down) (in children under six, hypoactivity)

(4) loss of interest or pleasure in usual activities, or decrease in sexual drive not limited to a period when delusional or hallucinating (in children under six, signs of apathy)

(5) loss of energy; fatigue

(6) feelings of worthlessness, self-reproach, or excessive or inappropriate guilt (either may be delusional)

(7) complaints or evidence of diminished ability to think or concentrate, such as slowed thinking, or indecisiveness not associated with marked loosening of associations or incoherence

(8) recurrent thoughts of death, suicidal ideation, wishes to be dead, or suicide attempt

C. Neither of the following dominate the clinical picture when an affective syndrome (i.e., criteria A and B above) is not present, that is, before it developed or after it has remitted:

(1) preoccupation with a mood-incongruent delusion or hallucination (see definition below)

(2) bizarre behavior

D. Not superimposed on either Schizophrenia, Schizophreniform Disorder, or a Paranoid Disorder.

E. Not due to any Organic Mental Disorder or Uncomplicated Bereavement.

Fifth-digit code numbers and criteria for subclassification of major depressive episode
(When psychotic features and Melancholia are present the coding system requires that the clinician record the single most clinically significant characteristic.)

6— In Remission. This fifth-digit category should be used when in the past the individual met the full criteria for a major depressive episode but now is essentially free of depressive symptoms or has some signs of the disorder but does not meet the full criteria.

4— With Psychotic Features. This fifth-digit category should be used when there apparently is gross impairment in reality testing, as when there are delusions or hallucinations, or depressive stupor (the individual is mute and unresponsive). When possible, specify whether the psychotic features are mood-congruent or mood-incongruent. (The non-ICD-9-CM fifth-digit 7 may be used instead to indicate that the psychotic features are mood-incongruent; otherwise, mood-congruence may be assumed.)

Mood-congruent Psychotic Features. Delusions or hallucinations whose content is entirely consistent with the themes of either personal inadequacy, guilt, disease, death, nihilism, or deserved punishment; depressive stupor (the individual is mute and unresponsive).

Mood-incongruent Psychotic Features. Delusions or hallucinations whose content does not involve themes of either personal inadequacy, guilt, disease, death, nihilism, or deserved punishment. Included here are such symptoms as persecutory delusions, thought insertion, thought broadcasting, and delusions of control, whose content has no apparent relationship to any of the themes noted above.

3– With Melancholia.

A. Loss of pleasure in all or almost all activities.

B. Lack of reactivity to usually pleasurable stimuli (doesn't feel much better, even temporarily, when something good happens).

C. At least three of the following:

(a) distinct quality of depressed mood, i.e., the depressed mood is perceived as distinctly different from the kind of feeling experienced following the death of a loved one

(b) the depression is regularly worse in the morning

(c) early morning awakening (at least two hours before usual time of awakening)

(d) marked psychomotor retardation or agitation

(e) significant anorexia or weight loss

(f) excessive or inappropriate guilt

2– Without Melancholia

0– Unspecified

OTHER FEATURES OF BOTH MANIC AND MAJOR DEPRESSIVE EPISODES

Age at onset. The first manic episode of Bipolar Disorder typically occurs before age 30. Major Depression may begin at any age, including infancy, and the age at onset is fairly evenly distributed throughout adult life.

Course. Manic episodes typically begin suddenly, with a rapid escalation of symptoms over a few days. The episodes usually last from a few days to months and are briefer and end more abruptly than major depressive episodes.

Most individuals who have a disorder characterized by one or more manic episodes (Bipolar Disorder) will eventually have a major depressive episode.

The onset of a major depressive episode is variable, the symptoms usually developing over a period of days to weeks; but in some cases it may be sudden (e.g., when associated with a severe psychosocial stress). In some instances prodromal symptoms—e.g., generalized anxiety, panic attacks, phobias, or mild depressive symptoms—may occur over a period of several months. It is estimated that over 50% of individuals with a Major Depression, Single Episode, will eventually have another major depressive episode, thus meeting the criteria for Major Depression, Recurrent. Individuals with Major Depression, Recurrent, are at greater risk of developing Bipolar Disorder than are those with a single episode of Major Depression.

In Bipolar Disorder the initial episode is often manic. Both the manic and the major depressive episodes are more frequent and shorter than the major depressive episodes in Major Depression. Frequently a manic or major depressive episode is immediately followed by a short episode of the other kind. In rare cases, over long periods of time there is an alternation of the two kinds of episodes without an intervening period of normal mood (cycling).

The course of Major Affective Disorders is variable. Some individuals have episodes separated by many years of normal functioning; others have clusters of episodes; and still others have an increased frequency of episodes as they grow older. Usually functioning returns to the premorbid level between episodes. However, in 20% to 35% of cases there is a chronic course with considerable residual symptomatic and social impairment. This is more likely when there are frequent recurrent episodes.

Impairment. In manic episodes there are usually considerable impairment in both social and occupational functioning and a need for protection from the consequences of poor judgment or hyperactivity.

In major depressive episodes the degree of impairment varies, but there is always some interference in social and occupational functioning. If impairment is severe, the individual may be totally unable to function socially or occupationally, or even to feed or clothe himself or herself or maintain minimal personal hygiene.

Complications. The most common complications of a manic episode are Substance Abuse and the consequences of actions resulting from impaired judgment, such as financial losses and illegal activities.

The most serious complication of a major depressive episode is suicide.

Predisposing factors. Chronic physical illness, Alcohol Dependence, Cyclothymic and Dysthymic Disorders apparently predispose to the development of a Major Affective Disorder.

Frequently an episode of Major Affective Disorder follows a psychosocial stressor. If an individual has recurrent episodes, however, subsequent episodes may occur apparently without precipitating factors.

Prevalence and sex ratio. Studies in Europe and in the United States indicate that in the adult population, approximately 18% to 23% of the females and 8% to 11% of the males have at some time had a major depressive episode. It is estimated that 6% of the females and 3% of the males have had a major depressive episode sufficiently severe to require hospitalization.

It is estimated that from 0.4% to 1.2% of the adult population have had Bipolar Disorder. In contrast to Major Depression, Bipolar Disorder is apparently equally common in women and in men.

Familial pattern. Major Affective Disorders are more common among family members than in the general population. This is particularly true for family members of individuals with Bipolar Disorder.

DIAGNOSTIC CRITERIA FOR MAJOR AFFECTIVE DISORDERS
BIPOLAR DISORDER

296.6x   Bipolar Disorder, Mixed

Diagnostic criteria for Bipolar Disorder, Mixed
Use fifth-digit coding for manic episode.

A. Current (or most recent) episode involves the full symptomatic picture of both manic and major depressive episodes (p. 208 and p. 213), intermixed or rapidly alternating every few days.

B. Depressive symptoms are prominent and last at least a full day.

296.4x   Bipolar Disorder, Manic

Diagnostic criteria for Bipolar Disorder, Manic
Currently (or most recently) in a manic episode (p. 208). (If there has been a previous manic episode, the current episode need not meet the full criteria for a manic episode.)

296.5x   Bipolar Disorder, Depressed

Diagnostic criteria for Bipolar Disorder, Depressed

A. Has had one or more manic episodes (p. 208).

B. Currently (or most recently) in a major depressive episode (p. 213). (If there has been a previous major depressive episode, the current episode of depression need not meet the full criteria for a major depressive episode.)

MAJOR DEPRESSION

296.2x   Major Depression, Single Episode

296.3x   Major Depression, Recurrent

> **Diagnostic criteria for Major Depression**
> A. One or more major depressive episodes (p. 213).
> B. Has never had a manic episode (p. 208) or hypomanic episode (see p. 209).

OTHER SPECIFIC AFFECTIVE DISORDERS

The essential feature is a long-standing illness of at least two years' duration, with either sustained or intermittent disturbance in mood, and associated symptoms. A full affective syndrome is not present, and there are no psychotic features. These disorders usually begin in early adult life, without a clear onset. This category contains two disorders: Cyclothymic Disorder and Dysthymic Disorder. Other terms for these disorders are Cyclothymic and Depressive Personality Disorders.

301.13   Cyclothymic Disorder

The essential feature is a chronic mood disturbance of at least two years' duration, involving numerous periods of depression and hypomania, but not of sufficient severity and duration to meet the criteria for a major depressive or a manic episode (full affective syndrome).

The depressive periods and hypomanic periods may be separated by periods of normal mood lasting as long as several months at a time. In other cases the two types of periods are intermixed or alternate.

During the affective periods there are signs of depression (depressed mood or loss of interest or pleasure in all, or almost all, usual activities and pastimes) and hypomania. In addition, during the affective periods there are paired sets of symptoms (see criterion C below). The following pairs of symptoms are particularly common: feelings of inadequacy (during depressed periods) and inflated self-esteem (during hypomanic periods); social withdrawal and uninhibited people-seeking; sleeping too much and decreased need for sleep; diminished productivity at work and increased productivity, often associated with unusual and self-imposed working hours; decreased attention or concentration and sharpened and unusually creative thinking.

Associated features. Associated features are similar to those of manic episode (p. 207) and major depressive episode (p. 211) except that by definition there are no psychotic features such as delusions, hallucinations, incoherence, or loosening of associations. Substance Abuse is particularly common as a result of self-treatment with sedatives and alcohol during the depressed periods and the self-indulgent use of stimulants and psychedelics during the hypomanic periods.

Age at onset. Usually early adult life.

Course. The disorder usually begins without clear onset and has a chronic course.

Impairment. Impairment in social and occupational functioning is usually moderate or severe.

Complications. See manic and major depressive episodes (p. 216). Frequently manic and major depressive episodes are complications of this disorder. For this reason some investigators believe that Cyclothymic Disorder is a mild form of Bipolar Disorder.

Predisposing factors. No information.

Prevalence. This disorder was previously assumed to be rare. Recent evidence suggests that among outpatients the disorder may be relatively common, the depressive and hypomanic periods being manifested by loss of interest or pleasure and an expansive or irritable mood rather than by acknowledged depressed and elevated moods.

Sex ratio. The disorder is apparently more common in females.

Familial pattern. Major Depression and Bipolar Disorder are more common among family members of individuals with Cyclothymic Disorder than in the general population.

Differential diagnosis. See manic (p. 208) and major depressive episodes (p. 213). When a **major depressive** or **manic episode** is superimposed on Cyclothymic Disorder, both diagnoses should be made because it is likely that the individual will continue to have Cyclothymic Disorder after recovery from the Major Affective Disorder.

Diagnostic criteria for Cyclothymic Disorder
A. During the past two years, numerous periods during which some symptoms characteristic of both the depressive and the manic syndromes were present, but were not of sufficient severity and duration to meet the criteria for a major depressive or manic episode.

B. The depressive periods and hypomanic periods may be separated by periods of normal mood lasting as long as months at a time, they may be intermixed, or they may alternate.

C. During **depressive** periods there is depressed mood or loss of interest or pleasure in all or almost all, usual activities and pastimes, and at least three of the following:

(1) insomnia or hypersomnia
(2) low energy or chronic fatigue
(3) feelings of inadequacy
(4) decreased effectiveness or productivity at school, work, or home
(5) decreased attention, concentration, or ability to think clearly
(6) social withdrawal

(7) loss of interest in or enjoyment of sex

(8) restriction of involvement in pleasurable activities; guilt over past activities

(9) feeling slowed down
(10) less talkative than usual
(11) pessimistic attitude toward the future, or brooding about past events
(12) tearfulness or crying

During **hypomanic** periods there is an elevated, expansive, or irritable mood and at least three of the following:

(1) decreased need for sleep
(2) more energy than usual

(3) inflated self-esteem
(4) increased productivity, often associated with unusual and self-imposed working hours
(5) sharpened and unusually creative thinking

(6) uninhibited people-seeking (extreme gregariousness)
(7) hypersexuality without recognition of possibility of painful consequences
(8) excessive involvement in pleasurable activities with lack of concern for the high potential for painful consequences, e.g., buying sprees, foolish business investments, reckless driving
(9) physical restlessness
(10) more talkative than usual
(11) overoptimism or exaggeration of past achievements

(12) inappropriate laughing, joking, punning

D. Absence of psychotic features such as delusions, hallucinations, incoherence, or loosening of associations.

E. Not due to any other mental disorder, such as partial remission of Bipolar Disorder. However, Cyclothymic Disorder may precede Bipolar Disorder.

300.40   Dysthymic Disorder (or Depressive Neurosis)
The essential feature is a chronic disturbance of mood involving either depressed mood or loss of interest or pleasure in all, or almost all, usual activities and

pastimes, and associated symptoms, but not of sufficient severity and duration to meet the criteria for a major depressive episode (full affective syndrome).

For adults, two years' duration is required; for children and adolescents, one year is sufficient.

The depressed mood may be characterized by the individual as feeling sad, blue, down in the dumps, or low. The depressed mood or loss of interest or pleasure may be either relatively persistent or intermittent and separated by periods of normal mood, interest, and pleasure. These normal periods may last a few days to a few weeks. The diagnosis should not be made if an apparently chronic course has been interrupted by a period of normal mood lasting more than a few months.

During the depressive periods there are some of the milder features of the depressive syndrome described as part of a major depressive episode on p. 210 (see criterion D below).

Associated features. Associated features (and age-specific associated features) are similar to those of major depressive episode (p. 211), except that by definition there are no delusions or hallucinations.

Often an associated personality disturbance warrants an additional diagnosis of a Personality Disorder on Axis II.

Age at onset. This disorder usually begins early in adult life, and for this reason was often referred to as Depressive Personality. Although it may begin in childhood or adolescence, in other cases it may begin at a period later in adulthood, in some instances following a Major Depression.

Course. The disorder usually begins without clear onset and has a chronic course.

Impairment and complications. The impairment in social and occupational functioning is usually mild or moderate because of the chronicity rather than the severity of the depressive syndrome. Therefore, hospitalization is rarely required unless there is a suicide attempt or a superimposed Major Affective Disorder. The complications are similar to those of Major Depression, although, because of the chronicity of this disorder, there may be a greater likelihood of developing Substance Abuse.

In children and adolescents social interaction with peers and adults is frequently affected. Children with depression often react negatively or shyly to praise and frequently respond to positive relationships with negative behaviors (sometimes testing, sometimes as manifestations of unexpressed resentment and anger). School performance and progress may be deleteriously affected.

Predisposing factors. Predisposing factors include chronic physical disorder, chronic psychosocial stressors, and another mental disorder, such as a Personality Disorder or an Affective Disorder that does not completely remit and merges imperceptibly into this condition.

In children and adolescents predisposing factors are the presence of Attention Deficit Disorder, Conduct Disorder, Mental Retardation, a severe Specific Developmental Disorder or an inadequate, disorganized, rejecting and chaotic environment.

Prevalence. This disorder is apparently common.

Sex ratio. Among adults the disorder is apparently more common in females. In children it seems to occur equally frequently in both sexes.

Familial pattern. No information.

Differential diagnosis. For a discussion of the differential diagnosis with **major depressive episode,** see p. 213.

When a Major Depression is in partial remission for a period of two years, Dysthymic Disorder should be considered as an alternative diagnosis to Major Depression in Remission. When a Major Depression is superimposed on Dysthymic Disorder, both diagnoses should be recorded since it is likely that the individual will continue to have the Dysthymic Disorder when he or she has recovered from the Major Depression.

Often the affective features of this disorder are viewed as secondary to an underlying **Personality Disorder.** When an individual meets the criteria for both this disorder and a Personality Disorder, both diagnoses should be made regardless of the causal relationship between the two. This disorder is particularly common in individuals with Borderline, Histrionic and Dependent Personality Disorders.

Normal fluctuations of mood are not as frequent or severe as the depressed mood in Dysthymic Disorder and there is no interference with social functioning.

Chronic mental disorders such as Obsessive Compulsive Disorder or Alcohol Dependence, when associated with depressive symptoms may suggest Dysthymic Disorder. The additional diagnosis of Dysthymic Disorder should be made only if the depressed mood, by virtue of its intensity or effect on functioning, can be clearly distinguished from the individual's usual mood. In children Dysthymic Disorder may be superimposed on **Attention Deficit Disorder, a Specific Developmental Disorder,** or an **Organic Mental Disorder.**

Diagnostic criteria for Dysthymic Disorder

A. During the past two years (or one year for children and adolescents) the individual has been bothered most or all of the time by symptoms characteristic of the depressive syndrome but that are not of sufficient severity and duration to meet the criteria for a major depressive episode (although a major depressive episode may be superimposed on Dysthymic Disorder).

B. The manifestations of the depressive syndrome may be relatively persistent or separated by periods of normal mood lasting a few days to a few weeks, but no more than a few months at a time.

C. During the depressive periods there is either prominent depressed mood (e.g., sad, blue, down in the dumps, low) or marked loss of interest or pleasure in all, or almost all, usual activities and pastimes.

D. During the depressive periods at least three of the following symptoms are present:

(1) insomnia or hypersomnia
(2) low energy level or chronic tiredness
(3) feelings of inadequacy, loss of self-esteem, or self-deprecation
(4) decreased effectiveness or productivity at school, work, or home
(5) decreased attention, concentration, or ability to think clearly
(6) social withdrawal
(7) loss of interest in or enjoyment of pleasurable activities
(8) irritability or excessive anger (in children, expressed toward parents or caretakers)
(9) inability to respond with apparent pleasure to praise or rewards
(10) less active or talkative than usual, or feels slowed down or restless
(11) pessimistic attitude toward the future, brooding about past events, or feeling sorry for self
(12) tearfulness or crying
(13) recurrent thoughts of death or suicide

E. Absence of psychotic features, such as delusions, hallucinations, or incoherence, or loosening of associations.

F. If the disturbance is superimposed on a preexisting mental disorder, such as Obsessive Compulsive Disorder or Alcohol Dependence, the depressed mood, by virtue of its intensity or effect on functioning, can be clearly distinguished from the individual's usual mood.

ATYPICAL AFFECTIVE DISORDERS

296.70 Atypical Bipolar Disorder

This is a residual category for individuals with manic features that cannot be classified as Bipolar Disorder or as Cyclothymic Disorder. For example, an individual who previously had a major depressive episode and now has an episode of illness with some manic features (hypomanic episode), but not of sufficient severity and duration to meet the criteria for a manic episode. Such cases have been referred to as "Bipolar II."

296.82 Atypical Depression

This is a residual category for individuals with depressive symptoms who cannot be diagnosed as having a Major or Other Specific Affective Disorder or Adjustment Disorder. Examples include the following:

(1) A distinct and sustained episode of the full depressive syndrome in an individual with Schizophrenia, Residual Type, that develops without an activation of the psychotic symptoms.

(2) A disorder that fulfills the criteria for Dysthymic Disorder; however, there have been intermittent periods of normal mood lasting more than a few months.

(3) A brief episode of depression that does not meet the criteria for a Major Affective Disorder and that is apparently not reactive to psychosocial stress, so that it cannot be classified as an Adjustment Disorder.

INDEX

DATE DUE

The Library Store   #47-0106